T0163829

FEARING GOD

Praises for
FEARING GOD

Carlson's book *Fearing God* surpasses by far the many other books and articles that I have read over the years on "the fear of the Lord." All Christians, and especially pastors, will benefit greatly by the wisdom and insight contained in *Fearing God*.

—**Rev. Dr. Donald G. Miles**, senior pastor emeritus,
St. John's Evangelical Lutheran Church, Denver, CO

Fearing God is a life-changing and life-giving book. Nathan Carlson winsomely embraces the challenge of explaining the "fear of the Lord" in an encouraging and honest way. The words "Don't be afraid of God, fear him" are a plumbline for my thinking and now for my living. This book is a must-read for both the courageous pastor as well as the honest Jesus-follower. I am inspired by this excellent book!

—**Rev. Dr. Michael A.L. Eckelkamp**,
lead pastor, St. John's & Renewal, Denver, CO

Nathan Carlson brings fresh insights to an ancient message that our modern church desperately needs. In *Fearing God*, you will discover a concept that is vital to our Christian walk yet often neglected or misunderstood. This book provides a course correction that will set you on the path to walk in the favor of God with your eyes fixed on him. I give it my highest recommendation.

—**Dr. Marty Meyer**, founder of YWAM Idaho,
author of *Epic Faith* and *Mission Accomplished*

Our God is not a one-dimensional character. Likewise, His majesty and mercy are best encountered through several perspectives. Nathan Carlson, in *Fearing God*, effectively asserts that we have often diminished what it

This book is dedicated to Jenny, my lovely wife of thirty-eight years who has encouraged me every step of the way and is a wonderful example of a woman "who fears the Lord" (Proverbs 31:30)

CONTENTS

THE FRIENDSHIP
AND FEAR OF GOD

"The LORD would speak to Moses face to face, as one speaks to a friend."
Exodus 33:11

"The friendship of the LORD is for those who fear him."[1] What a strange thought to associate fear and friendship! If I am afraid of someone, in the same breath I would hardly call him or her my friend. Rather, I would shield myself and keep my distance. I would be on the lookout to make sure the person doesn't harm my family or me. I would be vigilant, wary, and suspicious of the person whom I fear, and I would take defensive measures. I may even beef up physical security to my home—more locks, deadbolts, and a security system.

On the surface, linking the fear and friendship of God makes no sense. Certainly, God does not want us to cower in terror of him. Jesus referred to himself as the Good Shepherd who tenderly cares for his sheep. That self-description hardly evokes feelings of fear. Yet, the Bible is quite clear: if we desire the friendship of God, it starts with properly fearing him.

But what does it mean to fear God? There must be something more to this idea.

Unfortunately, this concept is seldom taught in our churches today. When was the last time you heard a sermon or a Bible study that focused on the fear of the Lord? I have heard many sermons and lessons on God's love, compassion, care, tenderness, magnificence, sovereignty, standard of justice, and the like. But when it comes to fearing him, the silence has been deafening.

In contrast, the value of earthly friendships is often taught. Friendships bring rewards, joy, and laughter. In fact, studies by the Mayo Clinic have shown that friendships are good for your health and boost your confidence and self-worth, reduce your stress, and give you a sense of belonging. "Adults with strong social support have a reduced risk of many significant health problems, including depression, [and] high blood pressure."[2] One is never poor who has friends, for friendships are rich with cherished memories. When I think of my friends, many names and faces come to mind. I have childhood friends with whom I built a tree house, played sports, set up a photographic darkroom, and went fishing and swimming. I think of my college roommates and the many experiences we shared together. I think of the members of my family, my Bible study group, and my business associates.

Honestly, if any of us were asked to name our best friend, God would not spontaneously come to mind. But that is something God wants to change. He wants to have a friendship with us, but it must be on *his* terms and not ours, and curiously, it must include the fear of him.

Who is this God we are to fear? Jesus reintroduced his Father to the world with the affectionate Hebrew term *abba*.

Abba—This tender term of fatherly endearment is not commonly used in our culture today. When speaking to our earthly father, we may call him "dad" or "daddy" but seldom the common Hebrew term *abba*. The terms of endearment we often use and the *abba* of biblical times are similar, for they convey a childlike and emotionally intimate relationship between a father and his child.

Abba—It is a special name for a human father used only by members of his family. When his children call him abba, he has their undivided attention, and when he hears that word, whether or not he's looking at his child, he recognizes the voice, its cadence, its accent, its timbre, and its tone. The father knows that *his* beloved child is calling him.

Abba—This is often the first and easiest word uttered by a Hebrew child. The word begins as baby talk as the child mimics his or her father who so wants his name to be the first his child speaks. Over time, *abba* signifies a deep relationship that has developed between father and child. When the child is born into the family, a bond is forged and promises are given by the father to love, protect, nurture, and raise this child, who at first is completely unaware of such commitments. But, in time, abba becomes real to the child. Commitments made become promises kept.

Jesus of Nazareth referred to his heavenly Father as Abba. In the garden of Gethsemane as Jesus knelt in prayer, he cried out, "Abba, Father … everything is possible for you. Take this cup from me. Yet not what I will, but what you will."[3] He uttered these words as he struggled in physical agony, causing his capillaries to break and his sweat to mingle with his blood. In his study of the Gospel accounts of Jesus's prayer activity in Gethsemane, Bible scholar Curtis Mitchell concluded that "The language of this prayer pictures a small child crying out in desperation to His daddy in the most intimate language possible!"[4]

In his moment of greatest need, Jesus prayed to his Abba. But for many of us today, transferring this sort of relationship to our heavenly Father often becomes awkward. Some of us have had abusive earthly fathers— fathers who beat us, terrified us, or were out of the picture so much that our relationship with them was at best strained and distant. If that was your father, the idea of God as father may not conjure up endearing, loving images. It may even spark fear or disgust or disdain. You may be able to think of God in other ways, but the notion of father is something from which you distance yourself.

For those of us who had more caring earthly fathers, we still might find the fatherhood of God a strange notion. We cannot touch God or see him. We have no physical relationship with him. Is our spiritual relationship enough to make the idea of God as Father real, much less one that can be captured by such intimacy as abba, dad, or daddy? Or maybe seeing God as our heavenly Abba feels too uncomfortably close. After all, we're talking about a Being who has planned every day of our lives, whose thoughts of us are more numerous than the sands of the sea, and who loves and cares for us more than anyone else ever could. Is it too presumptuous for us to assume that we can have an endearing relationship with such a magnificent God? No, it isn't. The apostle Paul wants us to know that, through Christ, we are the Father's children, his sons and daughters. And that he has given us the Holy Spirit to confirm within us our new familial relationship with the heavenly Abba: "And because you are sons, God has sent forth the Spirit of His Son into your hearts, crying out, 'Abba, Father!'"[5]

For many Christians, the spirit of Abba needs to be awakened, or maybe even reawakened. The seeds of this awakening have already been planted if we have accepted Jesus Christ into our heart. The same Holy Spirit that resided in and empowered Jesus lives in us and that Spirit wants us to call our heavenly Father Abba. In fact, the Spirit is crying out within us to call out to the Father this way. The Holy Spirit wants us to know the Father as Jesus did—as a tender, loving, kind, and compassionate daddy who only wants what is best for us. As the prophet Isaiah wrote, "the LORD longs [expectantly waits] to be gracious to you; therefore He rises to show you compassion [his tenderest affection]."[6]

As wonderful as all of this is, the same Bible also tells us to "fear the LORD your God."[7] Fear the one we are to call Abba? Fear him who loves us and saves us? Aren't the fear and love of God mutually exclusive? It might seem so, and they are to many believers. But let's dig deeper into love and fear to see if they really do exclude each other.

Imagine that you drive to your favorite local grocery store and luckily find the best parking spot, the one right next to the handicapped spots. As you are getting out of your car, a stranger walks up and tells you that he needs your parking place and instructs you to move your car. You would probably be a little indignant. This is your favorite spot, after all. You found it, and you see no good reason to give it up.

Now, let's make one small change to the illustration. The stranger is wearing a police uniform. Although this police officer does not know you, has no prior relationship with you, and certainly does not love you, you would likely begrudgingly comply with his request because you recognize his authority. But your obedience would be rooted in fear—fear that disobedience would result in your detainment or arrest.

Let's change the illustration one last time. The man who approached you is not just a police officer. He is the chief of police, and he is your father, your abba who loves you. This is the abba who was in the hospital room when you were born and saw your first breath and heard your first cry. This is the abba who clothed you, fed you, and provided for you. This is the abba who counseled you, raised you in the Christian faith, and lovingly but firmly corrected you when needed. What would you do now? You would quickly move your car, not just because you recognize the legal authority of the officer who can ticket you for disobedience, but because you also recognize him as your loving father who only has your best intentions at heart, who has loved you since before the day you were born, who would never ask you to do something that was not in your best interest, and who would sacrifice his life for you. Although you may not understand the reasoning behind his direct command, you would unquestioningly trust that he is exercising his authority wisely and you would be well off to willingly obey.

Likewise, our God, the Creator of this universe, has awesome power and immense authority. Because of this he should be reverenced and, yes, feared. But he is also the one who knew our names before we were born. He created us and loves us. He always acts with our best interests at heart. And he even sacrificed his own Son and raised him from the dead so that we can have everlasting life through faith in his Son. He is our loving, heavenly Father, our Abba, who only wants the best for us. So we have every good reason to love him and adore him. And we have good reason to fear him. As I see it, because he loves us so much, we have no reason to be afraid of fearing him.

Let's go back to the illustration again. Notice how fear and love became intertwined when the identity of the police officer was also the earthly father who loves us. The context of family changed everything. This is the way it is with the fear of the Lord. The command to fear God can only be properly understood within the context of family—God's forever family. But many of you may still struggle with this concept.

Recently, my wife and I discovered a pile of trash that someone had dumped on our farmland. Among other things, the large pile contained new iron fence posts, sixty-fifth birthday cards extolling a wonderful man, and boxes with mailing addresses still intact. My wife suggested that I at least salvage the fence posts, but I would have nothing of it. The envelopes containing the cards displayed a house address that was only one-half mile away, so I decided to take a drive and anonymously talk with the birthday man's neighbors. They told me that the man and his wife recently retired and moved away, and that their home would soon be listed for sale. I called the home's real estate broker and had a nice but firm conversation with her. Although she was not responsible for the litter on my property, she apologized on behalf of her client and sent someone out the next day to pick up and haul off the trash.

Two weeks later, while helping my son with a backyard project, I found myself in a local home improvement store buying the same style of iron fence posts that had once littered my property. I thought, *How ironic!* Then God impressed upon my heart that I had missed his provision because I was harboring an offense. God knew I would soon need some fence posts, and he had them specially delivered right to my land! But I was so offended with the homeowner's actions that I missed God's blessing.

Because of past offenses, many people will take issue with the concept of the fear of the Lord and will therefore miss this wonderful blessing of God. Perhaps people with authority in the church have wielded their power in an ungodly way, thus instilling fear in you but not the proper fear of the Lord. Perhaps the fear of the Lord has been horribly distorted into a vengeful, tyrannical God who seeks to punish us. Perhaps your earthly father was a mean man who you feared, so now you want nothing to do with fearing a heavenly Father.

Whatever your personal story, do not miss out on one of the greatest blessings that God has given to us—the proper fear of him. As best you can, I ask you to set aside those offenses and consider how the love of God and the fear of God go together like a tandem bicycle. Given how much God loves us and wants the best for us, we need to learn how fearing him actually supports his love for us and our love for him. I recognize that you may have some obstacles to overcome to properly see and accept how love and fear can fit together. Nevertheless, God, in his great love, has instructed us to fear him, for that is in our best interest.

One day I had lunch with Antonio, a friend of mine, who had graciously agreed to review a preliminary draft of this book. "Nathan", he said, "My dad beat me unmercifully, and because of that, I have a difficult time believing God loves me, and now you want me to fear him?"

"Yes," I said, "Because you will never really understand the love of God without the fear of God, and you will never properly understand the fear of God without embracing the love of God. They are two sides of the same coin, and only the fear of God will keep us from sin and all of sin's horrible devastation."

Ancient Israel's King David understood this wonderful relationship between the fear of God and the love of God. He exclaimed, "For as high as the heavens are above the earth, so great is his love for those who fear him."[8]

Rooted in God's Love

Over ten years ago when I turned the age of fifty, thinking that I now needed help waking up, some dear friends gave me a rooster to add to our small flock of chickens at our hobby farm in Colorado. We named the new addition Colonel Sanders. At the time, I was under the mistaken notion that roosters crow as the sun rises and then quietly go about the rest of their day. Was I ever wrong! Like all roosters, Colonel Sanders started crowing about an hour before sunrise and then crowed incessantly throughout the day.

At the Last Supper, the last meal Jesus shared with his disciples before his arrest, Peter proclaimed with much bravado that he would follow Jesus anywhere and even die for him. But Jesus admonished Peter that before the rooster crowed, Peter would deny him three times. As Jesus had prophesied, Peter did deny Jesus three times to three different people on that very night. When the disciple heard the rooster sound off, he was reminded of what Jesus had said and wept over it.[9]

The Last Breakfast

Later, after Jesus's resurrection, the disciples once again shared a meal with Jesus, but this time it was on the beach at the Sea of Galilee. Jesus had already forgiven Peter, that much was certain, but Peter's restoration was not yet complete. Three times Jesus asked Peter, "Do you love me?" and each time Peter said, "Yes, Lord, you know that I love you," to which Jesus replied, "Feed my sheep."[10]

When I think of Peter's denials, forgiveness, and restoration, I also think of our rooster, Colonel Sanders, and what he taught me about crowing. In agricultural countries, chickens and roosters are everywhere, and the cacophony emanating from them in the morning and throughout the day is constant and unavoidable. So I am quite sure that, in the aftermath of Peter's betrayal, every morning Peter awoke to the sound of a rooster reminding him of his failure.

During that early morning on the beach, the sound was no different. The roosters were crowing. But now the object of Peter's betrayal, with his nail-scared hands, hands that had just prepared and served his breakfast, was sitting next to him. Amid the distant din of crowing roosters, Jesus asked one question three times: "Peter, do you love me?"

Why three times? Was there a tinge of uncertainty in Peter's voice or did it take three responses to finally rid Peter of his false bravado? Or perhaps the Lord, who had yearned for this moment of reconciliation, just wanted to hear Peter's beautifully contrite response and declaration of love yet again.

After their breakfast on the beach, I believe that Peter's response changed, and the morning's rooster crow came to remind him of Jesus's love and forgiveness. Each morning God's alarm clock assured Peter that the Lord's "compassions never fail. They are new every morning."[11] This would certainly bring Peter comfort, encouragement, and a drive to remain committed to Jesus no matter what.

It's also true that the incredible forgiveness that Peter received and experienced must also be accompanied by fear, for God's forgiveness is undeserved, was only accomplished through the death and resurrection of his only Son, and without this forgiveness we would live a life without hope and face an eternity of punishment and hell. Therefore, the psalmist reminds us:

> Lord, if you kept a record of our sins,
>> who, O Lord, could ever survive?
> But you offer forgiveness,
>> that we might learn to fear you.[12]

As Peter discovered, the proper fear of the Lord begins with our heavenly Father's forgiveness, love, and compassion. Through his gracious actions toward us, God teaches us about this tremendous gift of fearing him.

Have you experienced his forgiveness? Have you accepted Jesus Christ as your Lord and Savior and received his eternal pardon? Jesus, the Lamb of God who takes away the sin of the world, can wash away your sin as well. When that happens, we join his family, and God becomes our heavenly Father, our Abba.

Or perhaps you have already become a member of God's family but you need a fresh revelation of his forgiveness. All of us will have a difficult time understanding the fear of the Lord without first receiving his forgiveness.

Our heavenly Abba, thank you that you sent Jesus Christ, your Son, to take the punishment for my sin. I receive your forgiveness. Thank you for making me a member of your family. In Jesus's name, I pray. Amen.

POINTS TO PERSONALIZE

- On the surface, a fear of God and a love for God appear to be mutually exclusive, and yet in Scripture they complement and augment each other. Our loving heavenly Father is also majestic and holy and in the end will judge the people of the earth.
- The fear of God can only be properly understood within the context of healthy family. The police officer story illustrates this well: there is no reason to be afraid of fearing God.
- We should be overwhelmed with gratitude by the forgiveness God has given us, but this same forgiveness ought to strike terror into our souls when we consider the alternative: what would have happened to us if God had not redeemed us through his Son, Jesus Christ.
- We learn to fear God as we are stunned by his grace.
- God, in his great love, has instructed us to fear him, for he knows that is in our best interest.

 POINTS TO PONDER

- How does your relationship with your earthly father help or hinder your view of God as someone who is all-loving and yet also to be held in awe, reverenced and feared?

- Like the story of the rooster, Colonel Sanders, what are mementos in your life that now remind you of God's forgiveness? Do you resonate with the passage in Psalm 130:4 that says, "But you offer forgiveness, that we might learn to fear you"? If not, why?

- The proper fear of the Lord is a learned behavior. What are your hopes as you read through this book?

1

THE QUEST

"These are the ones I look on with favor: those who are humble and contrite in spirit, and who tremble at my word."
Isaiah 66:2

"Whom do you admire most and why?" That question was posed to online readers and received a variety of responses. Many people most admired their mother or father; others admired rock stars, historical people, inspirational political leaders like Abraham Lincoln or Martin Luther King Jr., public figures such as actors or actresses, and close friends. Some reasons for their choices were superficial; others were inspiring and heartfelt.

God's criteria are quite different. He doesn't admire millionaires or billionaires, or the famous or flamboyant. He doesn't swoon over actors or actresses. He doesn't idolize rock stars and celebrities—"those who are well-known for being well-known."[13] He doesn't put on any pedestal the well educated or measure someone's heavenly popularity by her number of Facebook friends or Twitter followers. No, God esteems and admires those who are humble, contrite, and tremble at his Word. The qualities that God admires are remarkably different than humankind's. He looks at the heart.

He esteems the meek and unassuming. He is not looking for the sinless saint. He is searching for the one who is aware of his own natural depravity and decadence and humbly and reverently admits this to God. The Lord is looking for the person who so reveres the divinely inspired Word that the simple reading of it sends shivers up his spine. When was the last time that happened to you? One commentary says that someone who trembles at the Lord's Word has "an habitual awe of God's majesty and purity and an habitual dread of his justice and wrath."[14]

The church in general struggles with the concept of the fear of the Lord but is quite comfortable with revealing a God of infinite love. A lazy approach to theology has a difficult time reconciling a God who wants us to both fear and love him. Like a lost, ancient language, the concept of the fear of the Lord has largely disappeared from the church's vernacular.

Although separated by thousands of years, all of the writers and prophets of Scripture possessed a common predisposition of fear, awe, and reverence toward God. When these leaders spoke and wrote, they did so with an innate awe of God that colored everything they said and did. Like someone who is unaware of his own verbal accent, these leaders spoke and wrote with a godly, reverential bias, often without even being aware of it.

In Scripture, the Hebrew and Greek words *yirah* or *yare*, *phobeo*, and *eulabeia* are interchangeably translated "fear, awe, and reverence," depending on the context. Primarily, however, they are translated "fear." However, the fear of the Lord is not so much a word defined in a dictionary but a personal predisposition toward the God of the universe. It is an ingrained attitude that outwardly manifests itself at different times as we fear, awe, and reverence God. Awe and reverence, however, differ from fear. They are not substitutes for or synonyms of the fear of the Lord. Instead awe and reverence are outward expressions of the fear of God.

The fear of the Lord is a bent or paradigm we have toward God. Distilling it down to a specific definition cannot be done any more than words can adequately describe the beauty of a sunset. So that we craft a well-rounded, scriptural understanding in this book, I will develop the concept of the fear of the Lord using all three terms but primarily using "fear" in keeping with Scripture and with Jesus's instruction when he admonished his disciples, "But I will show you whom you should fear [*phobeo*]: Fear [*phobeo*] him who, after your body has been killed, has authority to throw you into hell. Yes, I tell you, fear [*phobeo*] him."[15]

The Fear of the Lord in Scripture

Although the fear of the Lord has almost disappeared from the church today, it is one of the most foundational doctrines of the Christian faith and is found throughout the Bible. Here is just a sampling:

The fear of the Lord ...

Is one thing that Jesus greatly delighted in	"The Spirit of the LORD will rest on him—the Spirit of wisdom and of understanding, the Spirit of counsel and of might, the Spirit of the knowledge and fear [yirah] of the LORD—and he will delight in the fear [*yirah*] of the LORD." (Isaiah 11:2–3)[16]
Gives us contentment and rest	"The fear [*yirah*] of the LORD leads to life; then one rests content, untouched by trouble." (Proverbs 19:23)

Gives us protection and security	"The angel of the LORD encamps around those who fear [*yirah*] him, and he delivers them." (Psalm 34:7)
Grants us God's provision	"Fear [*yirah*] the LORD, you his holy people, for those who fear him lack nothing." (Psalm 34:9)
Bestows God's favor and blessing on all	"He will bless those who fear [*yirah*] the LORD—small and great alike." (Psalm 115:13)
Engenders God's tender compassion	"As a father has compassion on his children, so the LORD has compassion on those who fear [*yare'*] him." (Psalm 103:13)
Extends God's kindness and mercy to us and to generations yet unborn	"His mercy extends to those who fear [*phobeo*] him, from generation to generation." (Luke 1:50)
Reveals God's unlimited love	"For as high as the heavens are above the earth, so great is his love for those who fear [*yare'*] him." (Psalm 103:11)
Is life-giving and keeps us safe from satan's snares	"The fear [*yirah*] of the LORD is a fountain of life, turning a person from the snares of death." (Proverbs 14:27)
Is a prerequisite to wisdom	"The fear [*yirah*] of the LORD is the beginning of wisdom, and knowledge of the Holy One is understanding." (Proverbs 9:10)

Is the foundation for a healthy marriage	"Submit to one another out of reverence [*phobos*] for Christ." (Ephesians 5:21)
Ensures God's continued blessings to our children and grandchildren	"Oh, that their hearts would be inclined to fear [*yare*] me and keep all my commands always, so that it might go well with them and their children forever!" (Deuteronomy 5:29) "Whoever fears [*yirah*] the LORD has a secure fortress, and for their children it will be a refuge." (Proverbs 14:26)
Keeps us from sin and all of its devastation	"Moses said to the people, 'Do not be afraid [*yare*]. God has come to test you, so that the fear [*yirah*] of God will be with you to keep you from sinning.' " (Exodus 20:20) "Through love and faithfulness sin is atoned for; through the fear [*yirah*] of the LORD evil is avoided." (Proverbs 16:6)
Without it our worship is unacceptable to God	"Therefore, since we are receiving a kingdom that cannot be shaken, let us be thankful, and so worship God acceptably with reverence [*eulabeia*] and awe, for our 'God is a consuming fire.' " (Hebrews 12:28–29)

Is continually present in heaven and brings glory to God's name	"He said in a loud voice, 'Fear [*phobeo*] God and give him glory, because the hour of his judgment has come. Worship him who made the heavens, the earth, the sea and the springs of water.'" (Revelation 14:7) "Then a voice came from the throne, saying: 'Praise our God, all you his servants, you who fear [*phobeo*] him, both great and small!'" (Revelation 19:5)
Creates in us humility and gives us rewards from God as he sees fit	"Humility is the fear [*yirah*] of the LORD; its wages are riches and honor and life." (Proverbs 22:4)
Fills our spouse with life-giving richness and our children with healthy, personal growth	"Blessed are all who fear [*yare'*] the LORD, who walk in obedience to him. You will eat the fruit of your labor; blessings and prosperity will be yours. Your wife will be like a fruitful vine within your house; your children will be like olive shoots around your table. Yes, this will be the blessing for the man who fears the LORD." (Psalm 128:1–4)

Heals us emotionally and replaces our hurt with innocent, unbridled joy	"But for you who revere [*yare*] my name, the sun of righteousness will rise with healing in its rays. And you will go out and frolic like well-fed calves." (Malachi 4:2)
Provides an opportunity for God to eavesdrop on the conversations of those who fear Him, take notes, and pay special attention to their requests and petitions	"Then those who feared [*yirah*] the LORD talked with each other, and the LORD listened and heard. A scroll of remembrance was written in his presence concerning those who feared [*yare*] the LORD and honored his name. 'On the day when I act,' says the LORD Almighty, 'they will be my treasured possession. I will spare them, just as a father has compassion and spares his son who serves him. And you will again see the distinction between the righteous and the wicked, between those who serve God and those who do not.' " (Malachi 3:16–18)

The fear of the Lord is a common trait possessed by all great men and women of the Bible. As we will discover later, it kept Joseph from committing adultery with Potiphar's wife and kept Daniel from abandoning the Lord while living in captivity in Babylon. The lack of it was King Saul's downfall and almost ended the prophet Elijah's ministry. It birthed the world's greatest evangelistic outreach to the entire known world, is the goal of evangelism, defines acceptable worship, confers God's blessing, and was the one redeeming trait the thief on the cross, crucified next to Jesus, still possessed, resulting in his eternal salvation. It instilled courage in Shadrach, Meshach, and Abednego to stand for their faith, alone against the Babylonian emperor, and it has inspired millions of Christian heroes, such as Martin Luther, to do likewise.

It is one of God's greatest blessings but is seldom taught, poorly understood, and usually misinterpreted. It is foundational to sound doctrine and Christian maturity. We will discover how Jesus embraced it, taught it to his disciples, and how it is woven into the fabric of the Lord's prayer.

The fear of the Lord is mentioned numerous times in the Bible but seldom found on the lips of preachers and other church leaders. It was the one trait that God wished that each generation would give to the next. God told Moses at Mount Sinai, "Oh, that their hearts would be inclined to fear me and keep all my commands always, *so that it might go well with them and their children forever!*"[17] When God wrote out his inheritance list, he did not wish that we would just pass on to our children possessions, wealth, or knowledge. Instead, God wanted each generation to receive something far more important. If each succeeding generation is to experience the blessings of God—blessings that flow from us keeping his commands—the heart of each generation must be predisposed and inclined to *fear* him.

King David acknowledged that he was a descendant of a long line of men and women who were inclined to fear God and that he was a recipient of the generational blessings that God bestows upon such kin. Abraham, Isaac, Jacob, Salmon, Rahab, Boaz, Ruth, Obed, and his father Jesse were certainly not perfect, but their hearts had an inclination to fear God, which resulted in their obedience to his Word. God's commensurate blessings always follow obedience. That is why King David wrote in Psalm 61:5, "you have given me the heritage of those who fear your name."

I realize that fearing God is a tough sell. Aren't we supposed to love God and not be afraid of him? Didn't the apostle John write that "perfect love casts out fear"?[18] Isn't this concept part of the Old Testament and not the New? In the ensuing chapters, I will address misunderstandings that have grown up around these issues as well as several others.

For now, however, you should know that the quest to understand the fear of the Lord begins with acceptance—acceptance that the Word of God is living and active and is able to instruct, teach, and transform us into the image of Christ. As human beings, we naturally want to understand something before we accept it. However, in Proverbs 2, the quest to discover the fear of the Lord *begins* with accepting the authority of God's Word and *ends* with understanding the fear of the Lord.

> My son, if you *accept* my words and *store up* my commands within you, *turning your ear* to wisdom and *applying your* heart to understanding—indeed, if you *call out* for insight and *cry aloud* for understanding, and if you *look for it* as for silver and *search for it* as for hidden treasure, then you will *understand the fear of the* LORD and find the knowledge of God.[19]

Notice all the action verbs in this passage—*accept, store, turning, applying, call out, cry aloud, look,* and *search*—all culminating in understanding and finding. There is nothing passive about this quest. The very nature of faith means that God doesn't just zap us with the fear of him, like animals that have an instinctive fear of human beings. No, the proper fear of Abba is something that must be actively pursued and searched for like the hidden treasure that it is, using the treasure map that is God's Word.

Understanding the fear of the Lord and finding the knowledge of God happen together; one cannot know God without first understanding the fear of God. "The LORD confides in those who fear him."[20] Unlike a phobia, which is an irrational fear, the fear of the Lord is something we must deliberately nurture in our lives, for it is life-giving, protects us, guides us, keeps us, and is the beginning of wisdom and the knowledge of God. It is not an irrational, unreasonable fear. Rather, it's a rational, reasonable, and beneficial fear of him who is real, infinite, all-powerful, all-knowing, all-good, and supreme over all things.

And so, we begin this quest.

 POINTS TO PERSONALIZE

- Many of our responses are ingrained. Through the years we have become predisposed to certain attitudes toward God. When you think of God, what immediately comes to mind?
- God chooses his friends a little differently than most people. He looks for those who are humble and contrite and for those who fear him. Those individuals we would usually glance over, the meek and unassuming, capture God's attention.
- The fear of the Lord is explicitly mentioned or implicitly taught in every book of the Bible. It is a core doctrine of the Christian faith.
- God wants the fear of him to be passed on from one generation to the next, ideally from parents to their children. Repeat this verse out loud with the yearning and passion that was probably in the voice of God: "Oh, that their hearts would be inclined to fear me and keep all my commands always, *so that it might go well with them and their children forever!*"[21]
- It is unnatural for us to accept something before we understand it, and yet in Proverbs 2 the fear of the Lord begins with accepting

it and ends with understanding it. This can only be done through faith that the Bible is the inspired Word of God written for our good and that it must be obeyed.

- For better or for worse, our view of God is colored by our relationship with our earthly father. For some of us, this forms a healthy starting point; for others, this relationship is a great obstacle. Nonetheless, God wants all of us to fear, love, and trust him.

 POINTS TO PONDER

- God esteems those who fear him. He eavesdrops on their conversations, writes his thoughts on a Scroll of Remembrance, and calls these people his "treasured possession." Do you see yourself the same way God does? Do you see yourself treasured and highly esteemed? If not, why?

- Meditate on the many passages of Scripture in this chapter that mention the fear of the Lord. What conclusions do you draw from them about this bent toward God?

- What can you begin doing this week that will help you grasp, appreciate, and apply the fear of God?

2

OUR ABBA WHO IS IN HEAVEN

He [Adam] answered [God], "I heard you in the garden, and I was afraid because I was naked; so I hid."

Genesis 3:10

"Praise our God, all you his servants, you who fear him, both great and small!"

Revelation 19:5

One of the earliest chapters in the Bible begins with Adam hiding from God out of fear for his life, and the Bible ends with the heavenly saints who fear God giving him glory and honor. Scripture begins with a type of servile fear common of slaves toward their masters and ends with the fear, awe, and reverence of a mighty God by his redeemed servants.

So what is this "fear" anyway?

Why did King David sing, "The fear of the LORD is pure, enduring forever"?[22]

If the fear of the Lord is simply the fear of hell and eternal retribution, why does it exist in heaven where one's eternal salvation is certainly a settled issue?

In the book of Revelation, the fear of the Lord permeates the entire book. The angels, the twenty-four elders, and the four living creatures fall down in worship.[23] John the apostle fell at Jesus's feet as though dead. The saints in heaven who had been victorious over the beast were given harps by God, and they sang the Song of Moses: "Who will not fear you, LORD, and bring glory to your name?"[24] Angels instruct the saints in heaven to "fear God and give him glory, because the hour of his judgment has come."[25] After reading the book of Revelation, we are left with the unmistakable conclusion that in heaven this pure, eternal fear of the Lord that King David sang about is an instinctive and automatic response by all and that the fear of God and the worship of God are inseparable.

Yet for those who have *not* been spiritually born again, who have not invited Christ into their life, there certainly should be a fear of hell and eternal retribution. Jesus admonished his disciples to "not be afraid of those who kill the body and after that can do no more. But I will show you whom you should fear: Fear him who, after your body has been killed, has authority to throw you into hell."[26] As Christians, the actions we take must be inspired by a proper fear of the One who created the heavens and the earth and who will decide where every person spends eternity—in heaven with him or in hell with the devil and his angels.

The Bible vividly describes hell as a place of outer darkness, a fiery lake of burning sulfur, a place where the fire never goes out, the realm of the dead, the pit of darkness, and a lake of unquenchable fire where there is weeping and gnashing of teeth. It is a merciless place created by God for the devil and his demons to be eternally tormented day and night.[27] Yes, for those who have not entered into Christ's new covenant, there is good reason to be terribly afraid of hell.

When this power and impending wrath of God towards sinful men have been displayed on earth, many have fallen in fear on their knees in repentance. Such was the case with the famous slave-trader, John Newton. Newton was part of the crew of the ship *The Greyhound*, which bought slaves in Africa and transported them across the Atlantic to sugar plantations in the Caribbean. In 1748 on one of those trips, his ship encountered such an unusually violent storm that this veteran and vile seaman was afraid for his life. He realized that his death was imminent, that satan had already dispatched his demonic horde to drag him into the caldron of hellfire. With the waves crashing over him and the rain pelting his face like liquid daggers, in utter terror he knelt before his Creator and asked forgiveness for the life he had led. Later, he penned the famous hymn "Amazing Grace" and wrote the insightful words, "t'was grace that taught my heart to fear, and grace my fears relieved."

We might say that John Newton's fear was transformed from being deathly afraid of a God who had every right to send him straight to eternal damnation to a fear, awe, and reverence of a God who instead chose to love him and save a wretch like him. The slavish, servile fear of retribution was replaced with a wonderful fear of the Lord—a fear that exists within a family context where promises (covenants) have been made (a covenantal fear). In Newton's case, both fears served their purpose: one drew him to God and the other fear—the enduring, covenantal fear, the fear that is infused with the love of God the Father—sanctified his soul as he worked out his salvation "with fear and trembling."[28]

The Exodus 20/20 Insight

The giving of the Mosaic covenant and the Ten Commandments at Mount Sinai is the defining moment in Jewish history. Prior to Moses, there may have been no Scripture and certainly no Torah—the books of Genesis, Exodus, Leviticus, Numbers, and Deuteronomy.[29]

God called Moses to lead the children of Israel out of Egyptian slavery and back to the Promised Land that God had given to Abraham and his descendants. The children of Israel, possibly as many as two million Jews, left Egypt and crossed the Red Sea. Rather than heading straight to the land of Canaan by way of the trade routes, a trip that was perhaps a month's journey, God made an unexpected right turn and took them south into the desert and wilderness of the Sinai Peninsula. They would not see the Promised Land for forty years.

The children of Israel were not ready to receive the land God had set aside for them. Although they had just witnessed God's miraculous power when he sent the ten plagues against the Egyptian people, when he split the Red Sea so they could walk across on dry land, and when he destroyed the Egyptian army, the Hebrews had no Torah, no priesthood, and no traditions. They were twelve tribes of former slaves, a squabbling bunch of relatives, but were not yet a nation. They were the children of Israel, and they still acted childishly.

It took them three months of travel, but Moses and the other Hebrews finally arrived at the foot of Mount Sinai. First, Moses went up the mountain to hear God's plan. God told him that in three days he would come in a dense cloud and all the people would hear him speak. The Lord said: "You yourselves have seen what I did to Egypt, and how I carried you on eagles' wings and brought you to myself. Now if you obey me fully and keep my covenant, then out of all nations you will be my treasured possession.

Although the whole earth is mine, you will be for me a kingdom of priests and a holy nation."[30]

Moses instructed all the people to prepare themselves for God's self-revelation and the covenant he would establish with them. On the third day, Moses led the people in a procession out of their camp to the foot of the mountain. "Mount Sinai was covered with smoke, because the LORD descended on it with fire. The smoke billowed up from it, like smoke from a furnace, and the whole mountain trembled violently. As the sound of the trumpet grew louder and louder, Moses spoke and the voice of God answered him."[31]

From this setting, God gave them his covenant, which began with the Ten Commandments: "I am the LORD your God, who brought you out of Egypt, out of the land of slavery. You shall have no other gods before me. You shall not make for yourself an image … . You shall not misuse the name of the LORD your God … . Remember the Sabbath day by keeping it holy."[32] To these four, he added six more. God promised that if they kept his covenant, he would bless them for a thousand generations. But if they disobeyed him and broke his covenant, much like an earthly father lovingly corrects his child, he would discipline them.[33]

What was the people's reaction? "They trembled with fear." And they said to Moses, "Speak to us yourself and we will listen. But do not have God speak to us or we will die."[34]

Moses' response is very insightful. He told the Hebrews, *Do not be afraid*, God has come to test you, *so that the fear of God will be with you* to keep you from sinning."[35] In other words, "Don't be afraid of God, fear him; don't shrink back." Moses encouraged them to boldly approach the presence of God, knowing that God had made a covenant with them. The sheer terror that they felt at that moment would not do them any good if they did not understand that the fear that they felt was for their benefit, because it was the one thing that would enable them to keep God's covenant and not sin against it. It was a good fear, a covenantal fear, given to them by a God who loved them and wanted to bless them for thousands of generations. He wanted to make of them a holy nation, but that would require obedience to his law, something that he knew was impossible if they did not properly fear him—the One who carried them on eagles' wings and brought them to himself. The fear of the Lord is a wonderful gift from God.

By now the Egyptian people certainly feared God because of the wrath he had inflicted on them, but this was not a covenantal fear. They only experienced sheer terror. Similarly, the Jericho harlot, Rahab, told the two men that Joshua sent to spy out the land of Canaan that the peoples' hearts had "melted in fear"[36] because they had heard that God had dried up the Red Sea, allowing the Hebrews to cross on dry land. But the Canaanites' fear was sheer terror, not covenantal fear.

On the other hand, God had demonstrated his great love for the children of Israel by freeing them from four hundred years of slavery and had brought them to Mount Sinai where he instituted his covenant with them and gave them the means to keep it through a covenantal fear of him.

At this point you may concede that the fear of the Lord is taught in the Old Testament, but is it taught in the New Testament and did Jesus teach it? Was it part of Paul's writings and a teaching of the early church?

Jesus's Greatest Delight

When Jesus reflects on his time on earth, excluding the resurrection, what do you suppose are his highlights? What brought him the greatest joy? Was it the look on his disciples' faces when they kept finding one loaf of bread after another in their baskets when feeding the five thousand? Or was it the time that he scared the wits out of them when he came walking to them on the water during a storm? Certainly, raising Lazarus from the dead would rank right up there. Or how about the deep theological discussion he had with the woman at the well in Samaria? We don't have to guess at the answer. Scripture tells us where Jesus found his greatest delight. The words are found in a prophecy that Jesus fulfilled, words uttered seven hundred years before Jesus was even born:

A shoot will come up from the stump of Jesse; from his roots a Branch will bear fruit. The Spirit of the LORD will rest on him—the Spirit of wisdom and of understanding, the Spirit of counsel and of might, the Spirit of the knowledge and fear of the LORD—and *he will delight in the fear of the LORD*.[37]

The prophet Isaiah, speaking of the Messiah, wrote that one of his greatest joys and delights would be the fear of the Lord. Fearing his heavenly Abba was not something that Jesus did begrudgingly; it was something he enjoyed and one thing that brought him great pleasure. Fearing Abba brought him more happiness than walking on water, giving sight to the blind, raising the dead, or feeding five thousand people, and he conveyed this delightful relationship with his heavenly Father through his teachings, his parables, and his prayers.

Surprised by a Prayer

The key to understanding the fear of the Lord, Jesus's delight, is found in none other than the prayer he taught to his followers. It's best known as the Lord's Prayer, and it's recorded in two of the Gospels: Matthew 6:9–13 and Luke 11:2–4. Many of us have prayed this prayer thousands of times and never realized that through it Jesus taught a proper fear of the Lord to his disciples.

The prayer begins with the very tender address of God: "Our Abba [Padre, Father, Daddy God] who is in heaven." While God is our heavenly Abba, we have no natural birthright into his family. Rather, we have been lovingly adopted into his family through his Son, Jesus Christ: "he [the heavenly Abba] chose us in him before the creation of the world to be holy and blameless in his sight. In love he predestined us for adoption to sonship through Jesus Christ, in accordance with his pleasure and will."[38] Why Abba chose to adopt us is a mystery that we will probably never understand, even in heaven. Some things in life must never cease to amaze us, and this is one: when he could have lived anywhere in this universe, why did Abba choose to take up residence in my heart of all places?[39]

In the Lord's Prayer, the initial address, "Our Father [Abba]," is more than a term of endearment; it also recognizes the covenantal relationship between God and us. Elsewhere in Scripture, we are collectively called the bride of Christ.[40] We are family. We are all brothers and sisters who have been adopted into God's family. His covenant with us is a family covenant. God chose to enlarge his family far beyond Israel. He sent his only Son to make atonement for our sin. He sent his Holy Spirit to woo us to his love and give us the inclination to seek him. He chose to create his holy temple within us. God offers us the opportunity to join his family and enter into a covenantal relationship with him. This is the God we address when we pray "Our Father who is in heaven."

The fear of the Lord can only be properly understood within the context of a covenantal family. It is like a child who, on the one hand, deeply knows that her father loves her unconditionally but, on the other hand, knows that her father is to be deeply respected and honored and will discipline her for disobedience. Like a child's respect for her father, the fear of the Lord is an awesome reverence for God. Living in the fear of God means living in the realization of accountability to him. It means understanding that he is God, and we are his creation.

Only when this wondrous love of God, our Abba Father, that we will never, ever comprehend, is received can we move on to the next portion of the Lord's prayer: "hallowed be your name." This God who we just called Abba has a name that is to be revered; it is holy. He is not to be trifled with, and I must do nothing to bring disrespect and dishonor to him. Yes, I may call him my loving, heavenly, Abba-Father, but those words must be uttered with reverence, awe, and, yes, fear. This Abba, who tenderly bends down to listen to my prayer,[41] is the same God who struck Ananias and Sapphira dead for lying to the Holy Spirit.[42]

It is the Holy Spirit who gives us the desire and passion to keep God's name holy, for "he leads me in paths of righteousness for his name's sake."[43] We must follow our Good Shepherd on this path, knowing that this well-worn path was created by others who have likewise followed the Good Shepherd's lead and who are now a part of God's celestial "cloud of witnesses"[44] cheering us on.

Jenny Lee Riddle, through her song "Revelation Song," expresses the awesome nature of our God well when she exclaims that even the mention of Jesus's name can fill us with "awestruck wonder."[45] Are we filled with awestruck wonder at the mention of God's name? In Scripture, the Lord has many names—Elohim, El Shaddai, and Adonai are just a few. But the holiest name of all, Yahweh, the name given to Moses at the burning bush, was a name the Jewish people so revered that they came to the point where they refused to even utter it aloud. As in Riddle's song, they were filled with "awestruck wonder" at the mention of the Lord's name.

Our fear of Abba must exist within the context of our redemption. Why did God reach out to you or me? Why didn't Abba just start over? Why didn't he change his own rules? Why didn't he waive a wand and make us sinless and then there would be nothing left to forgive? Why was God so captivated by his creation that he devised a redemption plan, spanning thousands of years, requiring the torture and death of his own Son, to fulfill a punishment for our sin—a punishment that he instituted?

We must be amazed that an Abba this powerful set his wonderful affection on us. Unlike the angels who sinned and were cast out of heaven to be eventually tortured in hell for eternity, Abba chose to redeem us. King David marveled at his redemption when he wrote, "If You, LORD, were to keep account of guilty deeds, LORD, who could stand? But there is forgiveness with You, *so that You may be revered [feared].*"[46] We can never really understand the incredible love and grace of God; we can only accept it and always fear the loving Abba who chose to forgive us.

The apostle Paul admonished us not to regress into that servile, slavish fear of God, for we have not "received a spirit of slavery leading to fear again," but we "have received a spirit of adoption as sons and daughters by which we cry out, 'Abba! Father!' "[47] Every time we pray the prayer that Jesus taught us, it begins with Our Abba. God never wants us to forget that we are part of his family.

Once we know "Our Abba who is in heaven," once Abba's love has captivated our heart, once his name is hallowed and what we do and say brings reverence and awe to his most holy name, we have finally found the fear of the Lord—the proper fear of Abba. Only then does the rest of the Lord's Prayer fit. We can trustingly say, "Thy kingdom come, thy will be done on earth as it is in heaven." We can receive from Abba the forgiveness of our sins that he "may be feared." And this loving Abba, whose name is hallowed, is the One who can be implicitly trusted to be right and good.

But trusting God is not a normal human response. On the surface it makes no sense to trust our lives, future, career, marriage, and children to someone who is unseen that we have never physically met. (Before we ever entrusted our children to a new babysitter, we first met and interviewed that individual!) But we are admonished nevertheless to "Trust in the LORD with all your heart and lean not on your own understanding; in all your ways submit to him, and he will make your paths straight."[48]

A trust in God is not itself an emotion but a natural outcome of two emotions directed toward God: the love of him and the fear of him. Someone who struggles with trusting God wrestles in one or both of these areas. It seems contrary to think that trust in God stems from understanding and receiving the overwhelming love of God while also comprehending that this God is infinitely and incredibly powerful and therefore someone to be awed and feared. It seems counterintuitive that trust emanates from the love and fear of God. Typically, when we fear someone, we do not trust that person. But just as two physical elements, hydrogen and oxygen, combine to create water (H^2O), so two spiritual elements, the love of God and the fear of God, combine to create a trust in God.

Who wouldn't trust a God with the power to create this beautiful world, with its birds, plants, animals, and people? A God who also loves us so much that he refused to spare his only Son in order to redeem us? That is the God we can trust, love, believe in, and yes, fear. Like Jesus, we can joyfully submit our will to Abba's will, and the fear of the Lord can become our greatest delight.

One Message, Two Truths

"One thing God has spoken, two things I have heard: 'Power belongs to you, God, and with you, Lord, is unfailing love'; and 'You reward everyone according to what they have done.' "[49] God speaks one message, but two things are heard. With one voice and at one time, God imparts two truths: he is powerful, and he is loving. God's greatness, his majesty, his strength, and his might cannot be separated from his love and compassion.

One message is spoken but two are received: God is great, and God is good. These two truths are inseparable, and one cannot be understood without the other. Only after this dual message is received can one make the trusting statement, "You reward everyone according to what they have done." In the end, God will balance the scales of justice; I need not become disillusioned when evildoers act with seeming impunity or the righteous are not rewarded but persecuted. Once again, the fear of God and the love of God create a trust in God.

> One God, one Lord
> One Spirit, one Word
> One message is spoken
> Two truths are heard
> God is great and God is good
> Trustworthy strength now understood.

> Blended together, one becomes two
> Majesty seen in compassionate hue
> Marvelous justice, justifying love
> God is fearfully awesome
> We are greatly beloved.

 ## POINTS TO PERSONALIZE

- The fear of the Lord is a blessing and a gift from God and is essential if we are going to not live a sinful life. We must not be afraid of God, but we must properly fear him. *"Do not be afraid.*

God has come to test you, *so that the fear of God will be with you to keep you from sinning.*"[50]

- Our relationship with our earthly father is usually the lens through which we view our heavenly Father, for better or for worse, but all earthly fathers are imperfect and therefore this relationship creates an imperfect picture of God. Nevertheless, God reveals himself to us through his Word, and as we begin to accept his love and authority without question, we also develop a proper fear of him.

- Jesus delighted in the fear of the Lord and taught it to his disciples in the Lord's Prayer. If our spiritual goal is to become more like Christ, then our fear of the Lord must grow and mature as well.

 POINTS TO PONDER

- When we are afraid of something, we naturally withdraw from it and seek protection. Yet, the proper fear of the Lord does just the opposite; it creates trust and draws us to God. Why is this so?

- Martin Luther wrote that we should "fear, love, and trust God above all things."[51] How are fear, love, and trust related and dependent upon each other when it comes to our relationship with God? Can we have a proper fear of God without also understanding his love for us and how the fear *of* God and a love *for* God develop a trust *in* God? Explain your answer.

3

FLYING WITH NO DUCT TAPE

Therefore, my dear friends, as you have always obeyed—not only in my
presence, but now much more in my absence—continue to work out
your salvation with fear and trembling, for it is God who works in you
to will and to act in order to fulfill his good purpose.

Philippians 2:12–13

On October 2, 1996, Aero Peru flight 603, a Boeing 757, took off after midnight on a moonless night from Lima, Peru, with sixty-one passengers and nine crewmembers. Shortly after takeoff, the pilots discovered that none of the basic flight instruments were working properly and the data they were receiving was false. Unable to properly determine air speed or altitude, the crew requested an emergency return to the airport. Despite a valiant effort by the pilots, with no moon, no working instruments, and no visual aids, the plane crashed into the ocean killing all on board. Upon investigation, it was discovered that a maintenance crewman had not removed the duct tape from the static ports of the plane that he had applied when cleaning the craft's exterior. These static ports are vital to the plane's operation since they are in many ways the eyes and ears of the aircraft and transmit key flight data to the pilots and the onboard computer. With the static ports taped over, unbeknown to the pilots, the flight instruments were displaying false data, creating a deadly and tragic situation.

Beware of Duct Tape!

God catches his fish and then he cleans them; salvation is followed by sanctification. God loved us so much that he sent his Son to save us, but God also wants to transform us from the inside out. That is called sanctification. Sanctification is a cleaning process that begins as we navigate our Christian life, but if we attempt to do this without the fear of God in our lives, it is as if we placed duct tape on our spiritual navigation port. The fear of God removes that duct tape and gives us a safe flight path.

Without the fear of God, we will not properly esteem God's Word; we will not choose to humble ourselves; we will not come to grips with the gravity of our sin and the wickedness of our sinful nature. We may not apologize for wrongful acts nor ask forgiveness of others; instead we will make excuses for our bad behavior: "That is just who I am." Without the fear of God, our finite mind will question God's infinite wisdom. Without the fear of God, we will think preposterous thoughts: *If I were running this universe, I would do things a little differently!* Or, *I think God could use a little of my advice right now.* In short, without the fear of God, our faith will not mature, and our inner life will not be transformed by the Holy Spirit. Beware of duct tape!

This is why Paul, in his letter to the Philippian church, instructs us to "work out our salvation with fear and trembling."[52] Or, put another way, we are to work out (and continue to work out) our salvation with fear and trembling. The Greek verb tense that is used implies an ongoing and never-ending process. Although salvation is a momentary event, through the power of the Holy Spirit at work within us, a salvation "workout" (sanctification) is expected, takes a lifetime, and is not optional. Once we have come to faith in Christ, our faith still needs to mature and develop within us. While having a fear of Abba, we still must wrestle with the applicability of that faith to our everyday life. As part of this, we must develop a biblical worldview that is shaped by Scripture and is not afraid to answer tough questions, such as: Where is God when I hurt? Are science and Scripture supportive or fundamentally at odds with each other? Is God just and fair? How do we reconcile the suffering in the world with an all-powerful God? Where is heaven and who gets in? Is the Bible God's inspired Word or are the stories myths?

The damage that a duct-tape approach to reality can take is clearly demonstrated by the lives of three men: Charles Darwin, Friedrich Nietzsche, and Joseph Stalin. Each man shows what happens when the fear of God is abandoned and replaced with ideas and approaches to life that cannot overcome what has been lost.

Charles Darwin was a British naturalist who penned the theory of natural evolution. Friedrich Nietzsche was a German philosopher and writer who proclaimed to the world that God is dead. And Joseph Stalin was a ruthless, violent, Russian dictator responsible for at least twenty million Russian deaths. All three men have this in common: they all intended at one point to enter the Christian ministry, and all three pursued this ambition by enrolling in a theological school! Darwin enrolled as a theology student in 1827 at Christ's College, Cambridge[53]; Nietzsche enrolled as a theology student in 1864 at the University in Bonn; and Stalin enrolled at the Tiflis Theological Seminary in 1894. Later, all three men not only rejected God but also ended up destroying the faith of perhaps billions of people and changing the course of history.

Interestingly, all three of these individuals walked similar paths away from God.

The Wreckage of Duct Tape

Darwin and Evolution

Charles Darwin's father hoped that his son would follow in his footsteps and become a doctor. However, Charles withdrew from these medical studies after witnessing the sufferings of patients who underwent medical procedures with no anesthetic, which had not yet been invented. His father then encouraged him to consider the ministry. Charles agreed to explore this idea and wrote the following in his autobiography:

> I asked for some time to consider [becoming a clergyman], as from what little I had heard and thought on the subject I had scruples about declaring my belief in all the dogmas of the Church of England; though otherwise I liked the thought of being a country clergyman. Accordingly I read with great care 'Pearson on the Creed,' and a few other books on divinity; and as *I did not then in the least doubt the strict and literal truth of every word in the Bible,* I soon persuaded myself that our Creed must be fully accepted.[54]

Accordingly, at the age of eighteen, Charles Darwin began his preparation for the ministry by enrolling as a theology student at Christ's College.[55] But within about ten years, Darwin had rejected Christianity, declared he was an agnostic, and began writing *The Origin of Species,* a book that would radically change the course of history. After this book, an increasing number of scientists no longer focused on discovering the awesome and fear-inspiring wonders of God's creation but rather sought to rationally show how religion had duped us into believing in a creator-God.

God? What God? God was no longer to be feared since his very existence could now be questioned and his marvelous creation explained away as a series of minute, gradual, biological changes over billions of years—changes not orchestrated by a Creator but through a process Darwin dubbed "natural selection," the "survival of the fittest." However implausible this explanation may be, the scientific community continues to flock to it for it gives them the spiritual cover they need. One cannot be an atheist without believing in naturalistic evolution.

How did Charles Darwin change from believing the "strict and literal truth of every word of the Bible" to the world's most famous agnostic? From ages twenty-seven through twenty-nine (1836–1839), Darwin served as a naturalist aboard the British ship *HMS Beagle*. He wrote in his journal:

> During these two years I was led to think much about religion. Whilst on board the Beagle I was quite orthodox, & I remember being heartily laughed at by several of the officers (though themselves orthodox) for quoting the Bible as an unanswerable authority on some point of morality. I suppose it was the novelty of the argument that amused them. *But I had gradually come, by this time, to see that the Old Testament from its manifestly false history of the world, with the Tower of Babel, rainbow as a sign, from its attributing to God the feelings of a revengeful tyrant, was no more to be trusted than the sacred books of the Hindus, or the beliefs of any barbarian.*[56]

After Darwin returned from this two-year voyage, he married his first cousin, Emma, a devout Christian, and began working on his theory of evolution. Darwin did not publish his theory for twenty years out of deference for his wife's beliefs. However, most scholars think that the death of his oldest daughter, Annie, in 1851 at the age of ten was one of the key catalysts in his decision to go ahead with the publication. Darwin was so distraught over her death that he could not even bear to attend her funeral.[57]

Strangely, Darwin turned to his own evolutionary theory to find meaning in his daughter's death, but his theory left him with only everything dies, and things die for no reason and no apparent end.[58] His theory told him that human beings have no soul or spirit, there is no eternal life, and his daughter's untimely death was an inevitable consequence of natural selection. In other words, according to his theory, his daughter possessed no eternal spirit, her death held no eternal significance, and therefore attending his daughter's funeral service was personally hypocritical.

The inevitable carnage from Darwin's godless theory had only begun. Jerry Bergman in his book *The Darwin Effect* writes, "As this book documents, his [Charles Darwin's] ideas inspired not only Nazism, but also communism and ruthless capitalism, costing the lives of an estimated up to one-quarter billion persons. Barrett et al has documented that in the last century 45.5 million Christians were martyred, a large number specifically by movements inspired by Charles Darwin."[59]

Nietzsche and Divine Death

I had already experienced so much—joy and sorrow, cheerful things and sad things—but in everything God has safely led me as a father leads his weak little child. ... I have firmly resolved within me to dedicate myself forever to His service. May the dear Lord give me strength and power to carry out my intentions and protect me on my life's way. Like a child I trust in his grace: He will preserve us all, that no misfortune may befall us. But His holy will be done! All He gives I will joyfully accept: happiness and unhappiness, poverty and wealth, and boldly look even death in the face, which shall one day unite us all in eternal joy and bliss. Yes, dear Lord, let Thy face shine upon us forever! Amen. (From Friedrich Nietzsche's private diary when he was age thirteen.)[60]

"God is dead." (From Nietzsche's work *Anti-Christ* when he was age thirty-eight.)[61]

Friedrich Nietzsche, one of the most influential philosophers of the nineteenth century, was born in 1844 to Lutheran pastor Karl Ludwig Nietzsche and his wife, Franziska, in Rocken, Germany, the heartland of the Protestant Reformation, just seventy kilometers from Martin Luther's birthplace. Pastor Ludwig, as he was known, was descended from five generations of Lutheran pastors.[62] Nietzsche described his father as "the very model of a country parson! Gifted with spirit and a warm heart, adorned with all the virtues of a Christian, he lived a quiet, simple, yet happy life, and was loved and respected by all who knew him."[63] Nietzsche adored his father and from an early age only aspired to follow his father's footsteps into the ministry. Friedrich was, in fact, referred to by his mother as "the little preacher" because of the volume of Scripture that he had memorized. To fulfill this lifelong ambition, once Friedrich had completed his secondary schooling, he enrolled as a theology student at the University in Bonn, Germany.

While there, he read Darwin's book, *On the Origin of Species,* and he began to be suspicious of the Bible that he had loved and memorized as a child. To him, Darwin's new theory was brilliant, and the Bible's creation account and the Bible itself were naïve. Ultimately, Friedrich Nietzsche concluded that the disciples and particularly Paul intentionally and fraudulently misrepresented Jesus's identity when they declared that he was divine. Jesus, concluded Nietzsche, was no more than a man.

Nietzsche became an atheist, an intellectual "high priest" of the atheistic movement, and famously declared "God is dead." By this he didn't mean that God had once lived and then ceased to exist, but that the belief in a God thought to be real was actually and finally culturally dead. The rest of his writings sought to work out the implications of God's nonexistence.

Stalin and Sixty Million Deaths

Speaking of Joseph Stalin, Bergman writes, "Like Darwin, he was once a theology student and, also like Darwin, evolution was a critical factor in transforming Stalin from a Bible believer to, for all practical purposes, a functional atheist." Bergman adds: "The importance of Darwin's ideas to Stalin's evolution into a communist is stressed by Parkadze, a close childhood friend of Stalin, who wrote 'in order to disabuse the minds of our seminary students of the myth that the world was created in six days, we had to acquaint ourselves with the geological origin and age of the earth, and be able to prove them in argument; we had to familiarize ourselves with Darwin's teachings.'"[64]

The books of Lenin, Marx, and Darwin "impressed him [Stalin] greatly," and he soon became an "avid Darwinian," abandoned his faith in God, and "began to tell his fellow seminarians that people were descended from apes and not from Adam."[65] In Stalin's own words, "Evolution prepares for revolution and creates the ground for it."[66]

Beyond a Duct-Tape Faith

Unable to reconcile new "scientific" teachings with Scripture, three men with apparently genuine Christian faiths rejected God and the results have been devastating. Although all three are long dead, the world's greatest atrocities have been self-justified through Darwin's theory; Nietzsche's books continue to be the "sacred writings" of the atheistic movement;

and Aleksandr Solzhenitsyn, the Russian literary giant, claimed that Stalin killed as many as sixty million Russians.[67] Atheism provides no obstacle to mass atrocities. After all, if there is no God, if nature is all there is, and if all of life is merely the product of random evolutionary processes, then life is by nature ruthless and meaningless, and natural forces favor the fittest and eliminate the weak. Why should society work against what's natural? Why should anyone?

If the fear of the Lord had developed in these three men, it would have kept them from their path of destructive disbelief. If Charles Darwin had feared Abba, in humility he would have searched for scientific answers that were in harmony with the Genesis creation account and would have found that sound scientific work and Scripture are not at all incompatible. In fact, recent research done by astrophysicists, as presented by Dr. Guillermo Gonzales and Dr. Jay Richards in their groundbreaking book and DVD *The Privileged Planet,* show how the universe and the existence of life on earth could only have happened through God's intelligent design. Two other DVDs by Illustra Media, *Unlocking the Mystery of Life* and *The Case for a Creator,* show how recent scientific research, when applied to Darwin's theory of evolution, prove his theory to be false using his own criteria. In his marvelous book *The Creator Revealed,* Dr. Michael Strauss explains how recent scientific discoveries of the origin of the universe align with a proper understanding of the biblical creation account.

We engage in a spiritual workout when we study God's Word, discover his truths, understand his character, and then apply all this to our everyday lives. We engage in this spiritual workout when we intercede for our needs and the needs of others, worship our Lord, receive his body and blood through Holy Communion, and joyfully share the good news (the gospel) with those around us. Working out our salvation is a vibrant and daily process of discovering new and marvelous truths in God's Word while holding on to and cherishing the foundational tenants of the Christian faith. Paul instructs us to "stand firm and hold fast to the teachings we passed on to you."[68]

However, as Paul also says in Philippians, the working out of our salvation must be done with "fear and trembling," and he would know.

While still a prosecutor of Christians and after the stoning of Stephen, Luke records that

> Saul [Paul's original name] was still breathing out murderous threats against the Lord's disciples. He went to the high priest and asked him for letters to the synagogues in Damascus, so that if he found any there who belonged to the Way, whether men or women, he might take them as prisoners to Jerusalem. As he neared Damascus on his journey, suddenly a light from heaven flashed around him. He fell to the ground and heard a voice say to him, "Saul, Saul, why do you persecute me?"[69]

Saul, an avowed terrorist of the early Christian church, thought that he was God's champion, called to wipe out the new Jewish cult called The Way, which was led by a man named Jesus who claimed to be God but could not even prevent his own death. Some God! This cult was a threat to Judaism, the temple, and the priesthood, and its membership was growing. Five thousand new converts had been added in one day on the Feast of Pentecost. Saul knew that this was the time to stop it by finding and killing its leaders. He saw himself as God's chosen vessel for this task. He was a Pharisee, and he had studied under the renown rabbi of the time, Gamaliel. Saul was blameless in his adherence to the Jewish law and probably had committed much of the key passages of the Old Testament to memory.[70] He had proudly participated in the stoning and death of Stephen, the church's first martyr. Saul had instigated the stoning of other men and women and had placed many others in prison, leaving their children orphaned and destitute.[71] Saul wasn't a misguided religious fanatic who happened to make a few bad decisions. He zealously led the orthodox Jewish charge against The Way, doing what the Jewish authorities had tasked him to do.

Now he was traveling to Damascus, Syria, a hundred-mile journey from Jerusalem and a foreign city, to capture, imprison, and kill more believers of The Way. As he neared the city, a terribly bright light, brighter than the sun, shown all around him, and he heard a voice from heaven, saying, "Saul, Saul why do you persecute me?" In terror he fell to the ground. "Who are you, Lord?" he asked.[72] He knew this heavenly being was majestic and powerful, an overwhelming splendor with penetrating brightness. He had no idea who or what this heavenly being was, but he at least knew to call him "Lord."

Then Saul heard the words that physically jolted him, sending shivers through his entire body. "I am Jesus, whom you are persecuting."[73] These first three words, "I am Jesus," changed the course of his life. In a split second Saul was transformed in his mind from being God's fervent and zealous champion who was purging and purifying the Jewish people of a blasphemous new heresy to the one who was inflicting pain and suffering on the supreme being he had just called "Lord."

He had murdered members[74] of the Lord's family. He had destroyed their homes, left them with nothing, imprisoned parents, leaving children without a mom or dad. He had watched the stones break their bones, rupture their guts, crush their skulls. He had destroyed communities and businesses. How could this be? How could he have been so wrong? He thought that he was righteously obeying God only to discover he was satan's hatchet man, a slayer, a grim reaper. He was fighting for God's archenemy and did not know it.

He had betrayed the Lord and had inflicted evil on thousands. Death and destruction followed him, and he had trained others to assist him.[75] He had developed a religious mafia and had cloned his terrorists. He was the leader of this pious and violent mafia that had sought and captured innocent followers of the Lord Jesus. The Lord had seen all his heinous acts and had watched as the life of his believers slowly ebbed away.

But it was worse than that. This Lord had himself felt the pain, for he said, "Why do you persecute me?" The pain of his persecution had been experienced in heaven by this Lord simultaneously with his followers on earth. The stones he threw[76] wounded the martyr and the Lord alike,[77] and he couldn't take them back. He could not reverse what he had done. The faithful followers could not be brought back to life, broken bones and bodies could not be healed, families could not be restored, and the sentences of those in prison could not be commuted.

Saul had been the leader of the group[78] that had brought false accusations against Stephen, and he was present when these charges were brought before the Sanhedrin, the Jewish ruling body. He had heard Stephen's speech before the Sanhedrin in which Stephen accused this group of murdering Jesus,[79] the Messiah, and had been one of those who, upon hearing this, rushed at Stephen covering his ears to prevent him from hearing further "blasphemy," shouted in defiance against him, and dragged him out of the city to be stoned. There Saul watched as Stephen's life slipped away as stone after stone pelted him and then he experienced supernatural love and forgiveness when Stephen prayed with his last breath, "Lord, do not hold this sin against them."[80]

When the Lord Jesus appeared to Saul, he told him to go to Damascus, the target of his planned attack, and from there he would be told what to do. But that wasn't so easy since he was now blind and had to be led to the house of Judas on Straight Street. There he spent three days in holy terror, in complete darkness, refusing to eat or drink.

This is the point in Saul's life (later named Paul) where he began to "work out his salvation with fear and trembling." This is the time that he reexamined all the Old Testament passages that he had committed to memory, except this time he did so with the fear of the Lord freshly imprinted on his heart. I am sure that he began his complete transformation with the firm conclusion that Jesus was the Messiah, was Lord, had risen from the dead, and was the Son of God as he claimed to be. Under the guidance of the Holy Spirit, the truth of Scripture transformed his heart as the prophetic passages came to light and he finally correctly understood all the messianic prophecies.[81]

With the fear of God in his heart, in three days his entire theology was transformed,[82] but there was still one thing lacking. He needed to be welcomed into the Lord's family of believers, and God had just the man for the job. In a vision, God mercifully showed Saul that his blindness was only temporary and that a disciple named Ananias would come, lovingly lay his hands on him, welcome him into the family of believers, and heal him. Perhaps the passage from Malachi came to mind: "But for you who fear My name, the sun of righteousness will rise with healing in its wings."[83]

Jesus did not appear to Saul at this time and heal him. Instead, he appeared in a vision to his faithful and obedient disciple, Ananias, who immediately replied, "Here I am, Lord."[84] Even before Ananias heard the nature of his new and potentially dangerous mission, he acknowledged his Master and Lord. And then he obeyed Jesus and went to the house of Judas on Straight Street that had given shelter to Saul of Tarsus. After entering the house, Ananias placed his hands on Saul and said, "Brother Saul, the Lord Jesus, who appeared to you on the road by which you were coming, has sent me so that you regain your sight and be filled with the

Holy Spirit." Immediately, "something like fish scales fell from [Saul's] eyes, and he regained his sight, and he got up and was baptized; and he took food and was strengthened."[85]

Ananias' first word to Saul was "brother," for he was now part of the Lord's family. Saul was now kin, and he was welcomed with open arms and brotherly love. Ananias did not attempt to validate Saul's experience. He did not question him to determine his authenticity. He embraced him.

To the astonishment of all, within a few days, Saul was in the Jewish synagogues proclaiming that Jesus was indeed the Messiah and proving this with scriptural passages. Then the hunter became the hunted, and Saul had to escape from Damascus with the aid of his newly found brothers.[86]

Like Paul, the formation of our faith must be done with the fear of God. When we ask those tough questions, when we read God's Word and discover his truths, when we forge our faith, when we worship and intercede, and when we partake of Holy Communion and share the good news, we must do so with "fear and trembling"—an attitude of profound reverence and awe toward Abba.

The apostle Paul told the Corinthian church, "since we have these promises, dear friends, let us purify ourselves from everything that contaminates body and spirit, *perfecting holiness out of reverence for God*."[87] Our reverential fear of Abba provides the motivation to obey his admonitions, follow his Word, and, like Jesus, delight in doing so.

Many people dismiss the need to fear God, equating it to a fear of God's eternal damnation of unrepentant sinners and therefore inapplicable to a born-again believer. In fact, they go so far as to say that someone who fears God has an immature understanding of his love and grace. Why fear a God of love?

Such ideas reveal a grave misunderstanding of this foundational tenant of the Christian faith, for not only did Jesus take great pleasure in fearing his Abba Father, but it says in Hebrews that Jesus's prayers to his Father were "heard because of his reverent submission."[88] It was only because Jesus joyfully chose to embrace a profound reverence and fear of his loving heavenly Abba that he also chose the extremely difficult Via Dolorosa, the Way of Suffering, that led to the cross and our redemption. His profound reverence for Abba is also what enabled him to pray in the garden of Gethsemane, "not my will, but thine, be done."[89] In short, if we want to become like Jesus and live with his kind of faith, we must properly fear Abba.

It bears repeating, "since we have these promises, dear friends, let us purify ourselves from everything that contaminates body and spirit, *perfecting holiness out of reverence for God.*" God's holiness in our lives can be pursued and embraced only with a reverential spiritual posture in our hearts. Trying to live a holy life without the fear of the Lord is futile since we won't have the proper motivation to obey him. Rather, the cleansing of ourselves from everything that is defiling body and spirit, thus bringing holiness into our lives, can only be done through the fear of Abba.

Jesus's fear of his Abba Father supercharged his prayer life and forged his obedient heart, which he *learned from what he suffered.*[90] Obedience is necessary for spiritual maturity and keeps us from sinning. "Through love and faithfulness sin is atoned for; through the fear of the LORD evil is avoided."[91]

Without the fear of the Lord in our everyday lives, we will attempt to navigate this Christian life with duct tape covering our spiritual, navigational "static ports." Without the proper fear of God, wreckage will ensue in our lives. For example, if we read God's Word without the fear of the Lord, we will cavalierly choose which truths to obey and dismiss those passages that challenge us. One of America's founding fathers, Thomas Jefferson, went so far as to construct his own version of Jesus's life, using a razor to literally cut out the Gospel passages he found offensive. According to an online article in *The Humanist* on Jefferson's Gospel version: "The virgin birth is gone. So is Jesus walking on water, multiplying the loaves and fishes, and raising Lazarus from the dead. Jefferson's version ends with Jesus's burial on Good Friday. There is no resurrection, no Easter Sunday."[92]

With the refining fear of Abba in our lives, not only will we obey him and stay far away from sin's devastation,[93] but we will also receive:

- God's contentment and rest: "The fear of the LORD leads to life; then one rests content, untouched by trouble" (Proverbs 19:23).
- God's protection and security: "The angel of the LORD encamps around those who fear him, and he delivers them" (Psalm 34:7).
- God's provision: "Fear the LORD, you his holy people, for those who fear him lack nothing" (Psalm 34:9).
- God's favor: "He will bless those who fear the LORD—small and great alike" (Psalm 115:13).
- God's compassion: "As a father has compassion on his children, so the LORD has compassion on those who fear him" (Psalm 103:13).
- God's mercy: "His mercy extends to those who fear him, from generation to generation" (Luke 1:50).
- God's love: "For as high as the heavens are above the earth, so great is his love for those who fear him" (Psalm 103:11).

Here is the good news: we are working out what God is working in. Philippians tells us that God is at work within us to will and to act in order to fulfill his good purpose. We are not working out our salvation alone. Rather, the Creator of this vast universe, who has chosen to make his temple within us, is molding and shaping our character from the inside out. As we read and study God's Word, partake of his Holy Communion, and worship him for who he is, the Holy Spirit is also working within us, giving us the desire to do those things, thus changing our character to be more like Christ—more loving, gracious, joyful, courageous, and patient.

The English Channel tunnel is an engineering marvel. It's an underground and undersea rail line that goes from England to France. It is about twenty-three miles long and at its deepest, two hundred and fifty feet down. An English/French consortium, TransManche Link, dug the tunnel with huge boring machines from two different starting points: one crew began in England and a second crew started in France. Because of exact engineering work, the two bores precisely met under the English Channel on December 1, 1990.

We are digging our spiritual tunnel from two directions: we are working out, while God is working in. We are reading God's Word while the Holy Spirit is giving us the desire to do so. We are praying for patience while the Holy Spirit is making us more patient persons. Some of us may be engaging in the scientific study of God's creation while holding in highest esteem the truth of God's Word that says, "In the beginning God created the heavens and the earth."[94]

Our spiritual workout must be done with an attitude of awe, reverence, and respect for our heavenly Abba, what the apostle Paul calls fear and trembling. If we don't see and approach God this way, the engineering on our side will be misdirected; the two bores will not meet in the middle, and we will not be aligned with the truths of God's Word. Without a reverence for his Word, we will be dismissive of its teachings, especially the more difficult ones, and we will pick and choose the precepts we wish to follow. Without an awe of God, we may conclude that he is mean and capricious when tragedy strikes the innocent.

We must admit that we are prone to apply duct tape to our spiritual static ports, thus creating rubble in our lives. We want to be self-sufficient and not dependent on God. We want to claim that our own human ingenuity and hard work have transformed this world without thanking our Creator who gave us the abilities to think and create, who planted in this beautiful earth the physical resources we need, and then made the laws of physics simple enough for us to understand ($e=mc^2$.)

Face it, we love duct tape. Our human pride says that we can live this life on our own, independent of our Creator. But our false bravado and spiritual chest thumping serve only to separate us from the God who made us and has the power to change us for the better.

The fear of Abba keeps our spiritual static ports clean and provides that spiritual north star to calibrate our moral compass. We'd like to think that we are naturally good and inclined to good deeds. The Bible says otherwise. It compares our "righteousness" to filthy menstrual rags.[95] But, with our moral compass properly calibrated by the fear of Abba, we will do those things that please our heavenly Father.

The spiritual flight path of Darwin, Nietzsche, and Stalin was a path of pride that led to the eventual denial of the very existence of their Creator. Today, many professing Christians are on this same path. Theirs may not lead to atheism and human atrocities, but it will lead away from all our Creator and Savior longs to give us.

Ultimately, there are but two paths: one leads to life, and the other leads to death. One ends in wisdom, and the other ends in foolishness. One is heavenly, the other is hellish. The one path is Jesus's. The other path is satan's. Darwin, Nietzsche, and Stalin followed the wrong path and changed history for the worst. A proper fear of Abba is what marks the other path, and it can change the course of history for what is far better.

POINTS TO PERSONALIZE

- Salvation is the starting point of our spiritual journey. God catches his fish and then he cleans them through a process the Bible calls "sanctification." Paul describes it as "the working out of our salvation." Our faith must mature, and this maturation process must encompass a posture of fear and trembling, for without it we will fall into deception and may eventually deny key doctrines of the Christian faith.

- The fear of the Lord guides us in this journey, much like the static ports on an airplane guide its navigational system.

- The apostle Paul wrote, "since we have these promises, dear friends, let us purify ourselves from everything that contaminates body and spirit, *perfecting holiness out of reverence for God.*" The fear of the Lord provides the proper motivation to obey God; it provides a reverential spiritual posture in our hearts.

- Although the Bible is not a scientific textbook, science and Scripture are not incompatible and the book, *The Creator Revealed*, by Christian physicist Dr. Michael Strauss, is highly recommended reading for those wrestling with this issue.

 POINTS TO PONDER

- Jesus said, "Anyone who chooses to do the will of God will find out whether my teaching comes from God or whether I speak on my own."[96] First, we must choose to do God's will and only then will we discover the authenticity of Jesus's teachings. Normally in life, obedience follows understanding; however, Jesus reverses that order. When it comes to following him, we obey to understand; we don't obey because we understand. Are there steps of obedience that you need to take? List at least one below and then prayerfully consider how you might implement it soon.

- Paul admonishes us to *"work out our salvation with fear and trembling."*[97] Have you forged your faith in a reverent posture, holding the inspired Word of God in high esteem or have you been cavalier and ignored, dismissed, or redefined its key doctrines to fit your own preconceived ideas of what God ought to do and say?

- Have you specifically made that choice today to do the will of God? Here again the Holy Spirit gives us that desire and inclination. You can pray, "Father, I ask that you will instill in me a love for your Word, a desire to do your will, a deep understanding of your incredible love for me, and a proper reverence, awe, and fear of you. I yield to you as my Lord, and I ask you to lead and guide me on this journey called sanctification. I ask you to be my North Star. When I stray from your path, I ask you to correct me and realign my steps. May I always honor you and obey you.

Help me understand your Word so I can apply it to my life. I ask all this in the name of your precious Son, Jesus Christ. Amen."

4

THE ANTIDOTE TO FEAR

The fear of man will prove to be a snare, but whoever trusts in the
Lord is kept safe.

Proverbs 29:25

It is only the fear of God that can deliver us from the fear of man.
John Witherspoon, signer of the US Declaration of Independence

Any quick search of the Internet uncovers hundreds of unusual fears: for example, epistaxiophobia (the fear of nosebleeds), alliumphobia (the fear of garlic), chrometophobia (the fear of money), and scriptophobia (the fear of writing in public). However, the most dangerous fear, the one fear that the Bible is most concerned about, is missing from every list—the biblical fear of man.

The fear of man drives you away from God; it prevents you from obeying God because the approval of man (mankind) is more important than the favor of God. The fear of man is a trap and a snare. Someone who fears man easily succumbs to peer pressure and is unwilling to take a stand for what is right. Minister and writer John Bunyan wrote that the fear of man is "the fear of losing man's favor, love, goodwill, help, and friendship."[98]

The fear of man is at the root of personal insecurity because we crave other people's approval. We are unwilling to speak the truth, for we seek the applause of man rather than the approval of God.

The fear of man keeps us from obeying God. The Bible instructs us to admit our faults, confess our sins, and pray for each other,[99] but the fear of man stops us from following God's Word. The apostle John writes, "Yet at the same time many even among the leaders believed in him [Jesus]. But because of the Pharisees they would not openly acknowledge their faith for fear they would be put out of the synagogue."[100] The Pharisees should have known better, but their predecessors had faired no better.

Let's look at two individuals from the Old Testament, both of whom knew more than enough to fear God rather than man and yet reversed the order. We can learn much from their mistakes.

Saul and God's Command

God's orders to Israel's King Saul were clear: annihilate the Amalekite nation, including their people and all of their livestock. Why the retribution? When the Amalekites attacked the vulnerable Hebrews in the desert shortly after they left bondage in Egypt, God promised retribution. Now, four hundred years later, the Hebrew nation of Israel was strong enough to act. They had a king, and they had an army 210,000 strong.

But King Saul did not obey the word of the Lord. Under the pretense of needing animals to offer to God for sacrifice, he allowed his troops to keep the spoils of war, the best of the Amalekite livestock. He also captured but did not kill Agag, the Amalekite king. When confronted with his disobedience by the prophet Samuel, King Saul said, "I was afraid of the men and so I gave in to them."[101]

We will either fear God or fear man; we can't do both. Proverbs tells us that the fear of man is a trap, a snare, something that trips us up when we don't expect it. The fear of man trapped King Saul into thinking that what he did was actually good. In his self-deception, he thought that he had improved upon the orders of God, for not only had he destroyed the Amalekites (or so he thought), but he was also sacrificing burnt offerings to God right out there on the battlefield!

Saul's disobedience cost him his kingship and the lives of his sons and had dire consequences for the nation of Israel. More than four hundred years later, Haman, a descendent of King Agag, an Amalekite and an Agagite,[102] attempted to destroy the entire nation of Israel. Only through the faithful obedience and actions of Queen Esther were the Jews saved.

Elijah and the Whisper of God

The famine in Israel, which had been prophesied by Elijah, lasted three and one-half years. Elijah had told King Ahab and Queen Jezebel that because of their wickedness, "there will be neither dew nor rain in the next few years except at my word."[103] But these rulers did not believe Elijah, and their wickedness did not change.

Famines are not your run-of-the-mill natural disasters. Unlike earthquakes and storms, they take time to materialize. They are slow and gradual. At first they appear as just a dry spell, and then as an extended drought. A crop failure every now and then is to be expected, but three crop failures in a row finally got the king's attention. He concluded that Elijah was the problem and had to go. Ahab made Elijah Israel's number one most wanted man. Rather than repenting of their wickedness, the king and queen wanted retribution against the prophet. Rather than falling on their knees and humbling themselves before the sovereign God who was powerful enough to control the weather patterns, they wanted to kill his messenger. So King Ahab searched the entire land looking for the prophet Elijah.

The famine, which was God's punishment to Israel for her sin, did not just affect Israel; it affected the entire region around Israel too. Sin does that. The consequences of sin extend far beyond the immediate sinner. The sins leading to divorce affect generations to come. The sins of hatred, greed, and lust destroy friendships and the consequences ripple out across many relationships. There is no such thing as victimless sin. What happens in Vegas doesn't stay in Vegas. We cannot sin in anonymity.

After three and one-half years, God instructed Elijah to provoke a spiritual confrontation. Elijah challenged King Ahab and 850 of his prophets of Baal and Asherah to meet him at the top of Mount Carmel in northwest Israel. With the people of Israel witnessing the contest, the false prophets and Elijah each constructed their own altar and placed wood and their animal sacrifice on it.

Elijah challenged the people of Israel: "How long will you waver between two opinions? If the LORD is God, follow him; but if Baal is God, follow him."[104] This contest would settle the issue. The prophet who could call down fire from heaven to consume the sacrifice would win.

Of course, the attempts by the prophets of Baal and Asherah were futile. But when Elijah prayed to the one true God, fire consumed the sacrifice, the wood, and the gallons of precious water that the prophet had poured on the altar just for effect. The people of Israel responded by killing all 850 of the false prophets.[105] Then Elijah prayed and asked God to end the drought, which he did. He sent rain to drench the parched land.

King Ahab's wife, Queen Jezebel, who was not at Mount Carmel, was not at all pleased with the contest's outcome and sent word to Elijah that his days were numbered; in fact, she was going to kill him within twenty-four hours. Although Elijah had just witnessed God's power and the tremendous miracles of fire and rain, for some reason her threat was able to rattle this great man of God and he fled over four hundred miles south, deep into the Sinai wilderness. There, while hiding in a cave on top of Mount Horeb,[106] the mountain of God, God told him to go outside and stand on the mountainside, for he was going to reveal himself to Elijah.

First, a "great and powerful wind tore the mountains apart and shattered the rocks before the LORD, but the LORD was not in the wind. After the wind there was an earthquake, but the LORD was not in the earthquake. After the earthquake came a fire, but the LORD was not in the fire. And after the fire came a gentle whisper. … Then a voice said to him, 'What are you doing here, Elijah? … Go back the way you came.'"[107]

Why the theatrics and then a whisper? After three fear-inspiring and awesome displays of God's power through wind, earthquake, and fire, God chose to speak to Elijah in a whisper. How ironic. Why? The words that God whispered were completely unexpected by the prophet. Rather than extolling Elijah's bravery at confronting the evil prophets, rather than thanking him for his faithfulness throughout three and one-half years of famine, rather than commending him for making the effort to travel four hundred miles to this holy mountain, God whispered, "What are you doing here, Elijah? … Go back the way you came."

What a shock! Elijah had walked non-stop for forty days and nights, nourished by angelic food given to him at the start of his journey. Through the hot and dusty trails, he had wound his way down to the foot of the Sinai Peninsula, covering his tracks all the way. I am sure that he was constantly scanning the horizon, watching his back trail to see if he could pick up a sign of anyone following him. He finally arrived at his place of refuge and sanctuary, a cave high up on Mount Horeb, the "mountain of God," otherwise known as Mount Sinai, the mountain where God had spoken and written the Ten Commandments and given Moses the law that Israel was now disobeying. Elijah finally arrived at this mountain, the most holy place on earth, only to find that he was four hundred miles off course! He thought he was smack-dab in the middle of God's will only to find out that he was so far astray. *That's not possible*, he likely thought.

Elijah had to think fast. Apparently, God did not understand the situation; God had not put two and two together and was unaware of the tenuous state of affairs; he did not know that if he, Elijah, was found and killed, God's entire spiritual plan for Israel was over, *kaput, fini*. God did not know how precariously close he was to losing it all! So Elijah stated what he thought was the obvious answer: "The Israelites have rejected your covenant, torn down your altars, and put your prophets to death with the sword. I am the only one left, and now they are trying to kill me too."[108] In other words, "God, I'm it. If you want your will to be done and your words to be communicated to your stubborn people of Israel, I must be protected because if something happens to me, well, it wouldn't be good. So, I came to your holy mountain where it all began. Here you can protect me because I am all you have left."

After Elijah had personally witnessed God's miraculous provision and protection for three and one-half years and after Elijah had seen the power of God consume his sacrifice on Mount Carmel and 850 false prophets slain, he wrongly thought he was the only faithful servant left. Like King Saul before him, Elijah had become self-deceived because he feared man. Elijah assumed that he was on the front battle line fighting alone. He didn't know that God had an army reserve. So God set him straight: "I reserve seven thousand in Israel—all whose knees have not bowed down to Baal and whose mouths have not kissed him."[109] Elijah needed a reality check, and God supplied it. Israel's salvation was not dependent upon the prophet, and he was not the last man standing. Man cannot thwart the purposes of God. The Lord is supreme, and he is sovereign. We are never the only one left.

Like Elijah, I would love to think that in some way God needs me to fulfill his plan and that I was created by him to meet this need of his. I would love to fantasize that I am so important that without me God's plans will fail. Of course, this would make him dependent on me and not me dependent on him. In reality, God does not need my obedience, worship, or praise. Rather, I need to obey and worship him. In fact, Jesus said that if we do not worship God, he is able to make even the stones to cry out[110] in worship. Here is the point. We must not delude ourselves into pridefully thinking that we are indispensable to God. God is indispensable to us, not vice versa. It is our honor and privilege to join him in his ministry on earth.

The prophet Elijah fled from Queen Jezebel's threats when he should have stood his ground. Elijah was absolutely of no use to God so long as he feared Jezebel's wrath. He needed to realize again the greatness and the power of the God whom he served. If he had, he would have realized that Jezebel's little temper tantrum paled in comparison to God's great power and sovereignty over all things. It is no coincidence that God told Elijah to "go back the way you came." The prophet needed to return to and confront his path of failure. He retraced his steps, knowing that each step brought him closer to the evil tyrant of Jezebel. But now he feared God, not her.

The wind, the earthquake, and the fire did not happen to teach Elijah how to hear God's still, small voice. Many times before, Elijah had heard and had recognized the Lord's spoken revelation. No, the purpose of the wind, the earthquake, and the fire was to display the incredible power of God to Elijah and rid him of the fear of man. God was to be feared, not Queen Jezebel. The same God who caused the wind, earthquake, and fire and who caused fire to fall from the sky and consume the sacrifice on Mount Carmel—that same God would protect him. Jezebel was not to be feared, only God. Elijah was part of God's covenant that included protection from enemies: "A thousand may fall at your side, ten thousand at your right hand, but it will not come near you."[111] But the prophet had forgotten this covenant. Before God could remind him, before he could re-disciple him, Elijah first needed to reexperience God's power. *The Lord makes his covenant known to those who fear him.*[112] Without the proper fear of the Lord, we will never become a true disciple. Without the proper fear of the Lord, we can never truly understand God's character, purpose, word, power, or even his love. The fear of the Lord is the foundation of discipleship, and we will never fully understand his covenants without it.

Elijah only heard God's still, small voice *after he feared God.* "The LORD confides in those who fear him, he makes his covenant known to them."[113]

The fierce earthquake, wind, and fire were necessary so that Elijah could regain a proper fear of the Lord, for only then could he hear and obey God's still, small voice. God wants us to fear him so that we can hear his whisper, so that he can confide in us. God wants us to be close to him, close enough and vulnerable enough to perceive a voice speaking specifically to us that is instructing, directing, and warning us, a voice that is imperceptible to others. Godly fear draws us to God but in a reverential way, not away from him. When we fear him, only then can we hear his whisper.

Elijah needed to fear God so he would depend on God and finally be at the place where he could hear God again. But he also needed to fear God so he could regain his courage. On this mountain, the Lord gave Elijah new and dangerous missions: to anoint his prophetic successor, Elisha; to anoint the next king of Israel, Jehu; and strangely, to anoint the next king of Israel's enemy, King Hazael of Aram (Syria).[114] God knew that he would be using this king of Aram to punish Israel for the evil reign of King Ahab and his wife, Queen Jezebel. Because Elijah feared God, God confided in Elijah and showed him his plan.

When Elijah returned north, he did so with confidence in a supreme and all-powerful God. He no longer had to nervously check his back trail for he knew that God's goodness and mercy would be following him all the days of his life and that he would dwell in the house of the Lord forever.[115] He remembered that the "angel of the LORD encamps around those who fear Him, and rescues them."[116]

Elijah was also reminded of the great mercy of God. While the prophet was traveling on his southward path of self-deception and disobedience, God had supernaturally provided food for him that sustained him just as God had done for the children of Israel every day for forty years in the wilderness, even when they were living in outright rebellion toward him. Perhaps Elijah had looked down from his cave and had thought about the infamous day when at the foot of that same Mount Sinai, the Hebrews had asked Aaron to cast the idolatrous golden calf despite having eaten that very morning the supernatural manna from heaven that God, in his great mercy, sent daily. Perhaps he had sat there in wonderment, marveling at the amazing love of God and astounded that he had not seen and comprehended this before. But then he was reminded of what King David had written over one hundred years earlier: "For as high as the heavens are above the earth, so great is his love *for those who fear him*."[117] Now the mystery made sense to Elijah: God's deepest and greatest love is reserved for those who fear him.

So Elijah retraced those four hundred miles. He obeyed and traveled back the way he came. He had panicked and had been driven south on this path of disobedience because of his fear of man. Now he boldly and courageously walked north in the fear of God. His cowardly and debilitating path of fear and failure was now his reverential and invigorating path of fear and faith. The timidity, turmoil, uncertainty, doubt, discouragement, and self-deception were gone. He had experienced a demonstration of God's power and was returning to Israel a transformed man. He now knew that if he feared God, King Ahab and Queen Jezebel held no power over him. The angel of the Lord had set up a defensive perimeter around him.[118]

The prophet also now knew that he would soon leave this earth, and he knew whom his successor would be. But he also knew that the timing of this leadership change was entirely in God's hands. He was now back on God's path, trusting in God's sovereignty, enveloped by his love, humbled by his grace, confident in his plan, and fortified with his protection. He now knew that until God chose to invite him to enter his eternal home, his life was protected and would be sustained, no matter what any human being devised against him.

The antidote to the fear of man is the fear of God, for the fear of man can never coexist with the fear of God. But, as Elijah found, the fear of man is so strong, so dangerous, and so spiritually debilitating that only the fear of Abba can displace it.

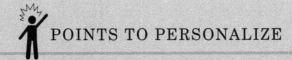 POINTS TO PERSONALIZE

- Some might rightly argue that certain fears are necessary and protect us. For example, a healthy fear of heights may keep us from dangerous situations. However, the biblical fear of man has no redeeming qualities. The Bible says it is a snare that will prevent us from obeying God.
- Exposure therapy is sometimes used to cure a personal fear. For example, someone with a fear of water may gradually expose himself to deeper and deeper water and eventually rid himself of the fear. However, there is no exposure therapy for the fear of man, and the only therapy or antidote is the fear of God.
- The fear of man is subtle and difficult to identify, for it often masquerades as peer pressure or an unwillingness to take a risk and do what is right.

POINTS TO PONDER

- What are some ways that the fear of man has manifested itself in your life? Don't be embarrassed about this. All of us deal with it. It's a common human problem.

- How would your response or actions have changed if, in those situations, you had feared God instead?

- What can you do going forward that will help you fear God rather than man?

5

COURAGEOUS FEAR

He fulfills the desires of those who fear him; he hears their cry and saves them.

Psalm 145:19

The remarkable thing about fearing God is that when you fear God you fear nothing else, whereas if you do not fear God you fear everything else.

Oswald Chambers

Elijah never again backed down. He did not flee; he stood his ground. After Queen Jezebel and King Ahab died, they were succeeded by their evil son, Ahaziah. At one point, he sent fifty soldiers to capture the prophet Elijah. Rather than fleeing to Mount Horeb, as he had done before, Elijah said to the captain and his fifty soldiers, "'If I am a man of God, ... may fire come down from heaven and consume you and your fifty men!' Then the fire of God fell from heaven and consumed him and his fifty men."[119]

Unconvinced of the power of God, King Ahaziah sent a second troop of fifty soldiers to capture Elijah and bring him to the palace, but they, too, met the same end. Unlike King Ahaziah, the captain of the third troop recognized the power of God in Elijah and pleaded with the prophet to spare their lives, which he did. Elijah allowed this captain to bring him to the palace where the prophet pronounced God's judgment on King Ahaziah.[120]

The Bible contains many paradoxes, including the last shall be first, and the greatest among you shall be the servant of all. Another is this: the fear of the Lord brings great courage. The fear of Abba, instilled in Elijah on Mount Horeb, gave the prophet the courage to confront the wicked king of Israel. This courageous fear is a common trait of every Christian hero.

Daniel, the Prisoner of War

The year was 605 BC. The prophet Daniel had every human reason to be bitter against God. After a lengthy siege, Babylonian King Nebuchadnezzar had captured Jerusalem and defiled the beautiful temple Solomon had built. He carried off to Babylon the holy gold articles from the temple and placed them in the temple of his god, Bel. Last, Israel's royalty and most talented, such as Daniel, a descendant of David, were removed from their homes, their families, and their land and taken as prisoners of war back to Babylon.

Daniel, a young teenager, had every reason to be angry with God. Everything had gone wrong. His home country of Israel was destroyed. The nation's temple had been ransacked and burned. He was separated from his family by a thousand miles of hot Arabian desert. He was forced to live in a strange land with a strange language, surrounded by weird, evil gods. He had been enrolled in a boarding school, "Babylon University," and asked to eat what he considered to be horrible, forbidden food.

Yet, Daniel did not blame God. He did not see himself as a victim. We know this from his own book, which begins, "In the third year of the reign of Jehoiakim king of Judah, Nebuchadnezzar king of Babylon came to Jerusalem and besieged it. And the LORD delivered Jehoiakim king of Judah into his hand." Daniel doesn't say, "Nebuchadnezzar conquered Jerusalem." In three short words we understand the heart of Daniel, for he writes, "the LORD *delivered Jehoiakim* king of Judah into his hand." From the opening paragraph in the book of Daniel, we understand that Daniel yielded himself to the sovereignty of God because he had a deep and abiding reverence and proper fear of God.

Daniel understood the power of God. He had been told of the many miracles God had wrought for the people of Israel. Daniel knew that the same God who destroyed Pharaoh's army in the Red Sea and killed Goliath with the sling of a little shepherd boy could easily have destroyed King Nebuchadnezzar's vast army but didn't. Daniel knew that God was in control and that he had brought Daniel to Babylon for a specific reason. He wasn't a prisoner of war. He was a servant of the Most High God who just had his entire mission trip to Babylon paid for, courtesy of King Nebuchadnezzar! He was God's ambassador to this evil empire cleverly disguised as a Hebrew captive. There was no questioning of God's wisdom, character, or purpose. And God didn't disappoint Daniel's faith and obedience. Daniel ended up serving at least six different kings of Babylon over a sixty-eight-year period, for God raised him to the highest levels of authority. Daniel achieved great power and influence during his sixty-eight years of public service, yet he was not consumed by this power because he knew that his ultimate allegiance was to the King of kings and the Ancient of Days[121] who reigned forever.

Only with the fear of God can one withstand the dangerous and spiritually corrosive influences of political power and remain a righteous leader. For example, when Nehemiah searched for a leader, he chose Hanani because "he was a man of integrity and feared God more than most people do."[122]

Because Daniel feared God he consistently made wise leadership decisions.

It was Daniel's courage, forged through his fear of Abba, that gave him the strength to ask for kosher food during his schooling and to encourage his three friends to do likewise.[123]

It was his courageous fear that gave him the bravery to stand in front of King Nebuchadnezzar and tell him that unless he repented the Most High God was going to drive him insane for seven years and he would eat grass like a wild animal.[124]

It was his courageous fear that compelled Daniel to disobey King Darius' edict and continue to pray three times a day to the God of Israel, resulting in him being tossed into the lion's den only to be rescued by the angel of God.[125]

And toward the end of his life after many decades of public service, it was his courageous fear that gave him the nerve to stand in front of King Belshazzar and all the nobles of his kingdom, reject the king's manipulative gifts, read the mysterious handwriting on the wall, and tell the king that because of his evil deeds, "he had been weighed in the balances of God and found wanting" and that the Most High God had taken away his kingdom and given it to the Medes and the Persians.[126]

Courageous fear forged through the fear of Abba is resolute, steadfast, and unshakable. It is an unwavering conviction that God's justice will prevail, whether in this life or the next; it is a firm trust that this powerful God, who transcends time and space and brought human life into this world with one exhale, loves and cares for each of us even more than the love he shows the birds of the air or the lilies of the valley; and it is a willingness to faithfully obey God's commands with a boldness born of these convictions. The world views these obedient acts as courage when, in fact, for the one who fears Abba, the safest place one can be is in the center of God's will.

As we will see in the life of Joseph, courage is an unwavering trust in God's sovereignty, even in the most difficult situations.

Joseph and the Audience of One

For the Christian, there is really no such thing as total solitude; we are always in the presence of the almighty God. Christian author Os Guinness in his book *The Call* discusses this truth. He writes, "A life lived listening to the decisive call of God is a life lived before one audience that trumps all others—the Audience of One."[127]

Like Daniel, Joseph also had every reason to be angry with God. His own brothers had sold him into slavery. Talk about sibling rivalry! After being sold as a slave, he probably walked bound to a rope for three hundred miles from Dothan in northern Israel, across the Desert of Shur in the Sinai Peninsula, and finally to the royal city of Pharaoh in Egypt. There he undoubtedly was placed naked onto an auction block, as most slaves were, and sold to his new master, Potiphar, the captain of Pharaoh's guard.

The Lord was with Joseph. He rose in responsibility and eventually was made overseer in Potiphar's house and over all Potiphar owned. Since Joseph was "handsome in form and appearance,"[128] he also attracted the unwanted sexual advances of Potiphar's wife, whom Joseph strongly rebuffed by saying, "How ... could I do this great evil, and sin *against God*?"[129] Notice that to Joseph the primary sin would not be against Potiphar or his wife but against God, his Audience of One.

All great heroes of the faith know that with God there is no anonymity. David wrote:

Where can I go from your Spirit?

    Where can I flee from your presence?

If I go up to the heavens, you are there;

    if I make my bed in the depths, you are there.

If I rise on the wings of the dawn,

    if I settle on the far side of the sea,

even there your hand will guide me,

    your right hand will hold me fast.[130]

The one who fears the Lord welcomes the comforting and continual presence of the Audience of One. And the one who fears Abba lives with great courage, for God's infinite power and boundless love are a settled issue.

It was Joseph's courageous fear that allowed him to rebuff the insistent sexual advances of Potiphar's wife, knowing that retribution might follow.

It was with courageous fear that Joseph used his God-given gift of interpreting dreams to tell Pharaoh that in seven years Egypt's fertile crescent, where the Nile—the longest river in the world—surrenders its rich silt, would cease to produce crops and a prolonged, seven-year famine would envelop that region. Yes, it took great courage to tell Pharaoh that one of Egypt's gods, the Nile River, would fail him.

It was Joseph's courageous fear that compelled him to forgive his brothers, for someone with deep bitterness and hatred could never have been such an instrument of God. Yes, early on, somewhere along that hot and dusty trail from Dothan to Pharaoh's royal city, Joseph chose to believe that his God was still in control, not his brothers, and that he was not bound by the cruel ropes tied around his wrists, but he was mercifully bound to God's unseen plan for his life.

Twenty-three years later, Joseph got to express this forgiveness directly to his brothers. The region was two years into the seven-year famine when Joseph's family living in Canaan ran out of food and his brothers were forced to travel to Egypt to buy provisions. Joseph was no longer the eighteen-year-old young man they had sold into slavery; he was now forty-one and had risen to be "father to Pharaoh, lord of his entire household and ruler of all Egypt."[131] Eventually Joseph revealed himself to his shocked brothers, and he immediately assured them over and over that this was God's plan. God had sent him to Egypt, ahead of them, to preserve them and to save many lives.

Then, sixteen years later, upon the death of Jacob, their father, Joseph again, in tears, reassured his doubting brothers of his forgiveness. He said to them, with wisdom, kindness, and grace born of the fear of the Abba, "'Don't be afraid. Am I in the place of God? You intended to harm me, but God intended it for good to accomplish what is now being done, the saving of many lives. So then, don't be afraid. I will provide for you and your children.' And he reassured them and spoke kindly to them."[132]

King David later wrote, "For as high as the heavens are above the earth, so great is his love for those who fear him."[133] God extends an extra measure of love and kindness to those who fear him. Joseph had experienced this love and, in turn, extended this to his brothers. Because he feared God, God's sovereignty became a settled issue in Joseph's life, never to be questioned. And from that grew an unimaginable courage, love, and wisdom.

Ruth's Courageous Fear

The touching story of Ruth, Naomi (Ruth's mother-in-law), and Boaz is one of the great love stories of the Bible. Because of a famine in Israel, Naomi, her husband, and two young sons left their town of Bethlehem and traveled east, across the Jordan River, and lived in the land of Moab for about ten years. The two sons grew up, and each married Moabite women, Ruth and Orpah. Tragically, Naomi's husband and her two sons died there, leaving three widows.

Naomi decided to return to her homeland and told her two daughters-in-law that they were free to remain in their land with their own people. Orpah returned home, but Ruth refused to leave Naomi's side and instead declared to her one of the most loving and beautiful vows in all of Scripture. Ruth replied, "Don't urge me to leave you or to turn back from you. Where you go I will go, and where you stay I will stay. Your people will be my people and your God my God. Where you die I will die, and there I will be buried. May the LORD deal with me, be it ever so severely, if even death separates you and me."[134]

So a broken Naomi and a loyal Ruth returned to Bethlehem after ten years. They were now poor, destitute, and hardly recognizable to the people of Naomi's village. It was the beginning of the barley harvest, and Boaz, a successful farmer, was harvesting his crops.

We are first introduced to Boaz as a "man of standing" within his community of Bethlehem.[135] He was an honorable man, a man of noble character with much land and many servants. He was also a kind and generous man who knew and followed the law of Moses. In Leviticus, God created a social welfare system that cared for the poor while still retaining their dignity. For example, the poor of the land were not simply given food. Rather, God instructed the farmers of Israel, when harvesting crops, to intentionally leave some of the stalks of grain standing to be gleaned by the poor.

Ruth happened to be gleaning in his field when Boaz arrived to check on how the harvesting was going. He noticed Ruth, discovered that she was the woman he had heard about who had refused to leave Naomi's side, and instructed the harvesters to be less diligent when harvesting—to leave extra stalks for Ruth, to protect her, and to give her water from their jugs. Then, at the end of the day, Boaz gave Ruth an additional ephah of grain, a ten-day supply. When Ruth returned home that evening to share this wonderful story, Naomi added another twist when she explained that Boaz was one of their kinsman-redeemers.[136]

When Joshua and the armies of Israel conquered the land of Canaan, it was divided out by tribe, by clan, and then by family. Although someone's land could be leased, it could never really be sold because every forty-nine years, in the Year of Jubilee, all land was returned to the original family. The land was passed on to successive generations through the sons that were born to the family. When a father died without any sons, the father's next of kin, known as the kinsman-redeemer, was required to marry the widow. The sons who were conceived would then be legally treated as the sons of the deceased father. The eldest son would inherit his land so that he and future generations would retain their land ownership and the sustenance from it.

Being the noble man of character that he was, Boaz knew this requirement but also knew he was second in line and that another man was Ruth's immediate next of kin. So Boaz assembled the elders of Bethlehem to clear up this issue. He explained that someone needed to step up, redeem this land, and marry Ruth. The nameless man refused to fulfill God's law, but Boaz obeyed. The rest is history. Boaz married Ruth. Together they had a son named Obed, who had a son named Jesse, who had a son named David. Yes, Boaz is King David's great-grandfather, and Boaz and Ruth are part of Jesus's lineage as listed in the Gospel of Matthew, chapter one.

However, a careful examination of Jesus's lineage also reveals who Boaz's mother was—Rahab, the harlot of Jericho who assisted the Hebrew spies who were sent by Joshua to scope out Jericho before the Hebrew army besieged it. The two spies found refuge in Rahab's home when they were being hunted. She told the spies the stories she had heard of how their God had dried up the waters of the Red Sea and destroyed the army of Egypt. According to Rahab, all the people of Jericho feared the God of Israel. But as it turns out, only Rahab acted with courage and with great personal risk to help the Hebrews conquer the land that God had promised them. She greatly feared the God of Israel and that gave her the bravery to hide the spies, give them an escape route, and then help them get out of the city.

Rahab later married Salmon who, according to Jewish tradition, was one of the two Jericho spies. I am sure that Rahab, Salmon, and their son Boaz, which means "in Yahweh is strength," visited the ruins of Jericho, seeing firsthand the remains of the walls that lay scattered on the plains. Boaz then heard the story of the city's capture from the two primary eyewitnesses now turned lovebirds. I am sure they took Boaz to the one section of the wall still standing where Rahab and her parents, brothers, sisters, and other family members had sheltered during the siege, and there they instilled in Boaz a fear of a sovereign God so powerful that he dried up the waters of the Red Sea and destroyed the walls of Jericho while lovingly protecting Rahab and her family. This God then brought a Hebrew spy and a woman of ill repute together and gave them a true love story. The fear of Abba gave Rahab courage and transformed this harlot of Jericho into a noble woman of God who raised Boaz to be full of courageous fear and an exemplary man of God—full of faith, wisdom, courage, and the favor of God and community.

The Fear of Faith's Heroes

Elijah, Daniel, Joseph, and later Rahab and son Boaz were separated by centuries of time. Daniel and Joseph rose to great power. Boaz was a small farmer in the obscure little town of Bethlehem. And Elijah was an itinerant, nomadic prophet. Their lives were so different, and yet they all possessed one common trait—courageous fear. And so it is with all great heroes of the faith.

What compelled the apostle Paul to travel over ten thousand miles on at least three different missionary journeys and have the courage to endure five brutal whippings of thirty-nine lashes? In addition, he says that:

Three times I was beaten with rods, once I was pelted with stones, three times I was shipwrecked, I spent a night and a day in the open sea, I have been constantly on the move. I have been in danger from rivers, in danger from bandits, in danger from my fellow Jews, in danger from Gentiles; in danger in the city, in danger in the country, in danger at sea; and in danger from false believers. I have labored and toiled and have often gone without sleep; I have known hunger and thirst and have often gone without food; I have been cold and naked.[137]

Paul reveals his motivation when he says, "Since, then, we know what it is to fear the Lord, we try to persuade others."[138] Paul's courageous fear of the Lord motivated him to forget what was behind him and to press on "toward the goal to win the prize for which God has called me heavenward in Christ Jesus."[139]

When the lowly monk, Martin Luther, was summoned to Worms to appear before the emperor and pope, surrounded by archbishops, princes, and dukes, to recant his writings that had exposed their corruption that had existed for centuries, he said with courage and conviction: "Take warning from the examples of Pharaoh, the king of Babylon, and the kings of Israel. God it is who confounds the wise. I must walk in the fear of the Lord." He concluded, "I am bound to the Scriptures I have quoted and my conscience is captive to the word of God. I cannot and will not retract anything, since it is neither safe nor right to go against conscience. I cannot do otherwise." Then he uttered those famous words: "Here I stand. I can do no other. God help me. Amen."[140]

At this event, Luther did not display a newly found reverence for God. This fear had been part of his being from the beginning of his theological training as a monk. For example, when Luther reflected on conducting his first Mass years earlier, after having completed his schooling, he wrote:

At these words [the liturgy of the Mass which, as the priest conducting the Mass, he was required to read] I was utterly stupefied and terror-stricken. I thought to myself, "With what tongue shall I address such Majesty, seeing that all men ought to tremble in the presence of even an earthly prince? Who am I, that I should lift up mine eyes or raise my hands to the divine Majesty? The angels surround him. At his nod the earth trembles. And shall I, a miserable little pygmy, say "I want this, I ask for that?" For I am dust and ashes and full of sin and I am speaking to the living, eternal, and true God.[141]

Author Eric Metaxas writes:

There isn't a historian the last five centuries who could argue against the idea that Luther's stand that day at Worms, before the assembled powers of the empire, and against the theological and political and ecclesiastical order that had reigned for centuries, and therefore against the whole of the medieval world—was one of the most significant moments in history. It ranks with the 1066 Norman Conquest and the 1215 signing of the Magna Carta and the 1492 landing of Columbus in the New World. And in its way, it far outweighs all those historic moments.[142]

Little did this humble monk know that his courageous words, born of his fear of the Lord and said that day before the amassed political and religious powers five hundred years ago, would upend the world as it was, launch a spiritual and political revolution known as the Protestant Reformation, and change the course of history and civilization.

 POINTS TO PERSONALIZE

- It is a paradoxical thought but the fear of the Lord develops within us great courage, and this courageous fear has been a common thread of all the champions of our faith.
- When we fear God, our perspective changes. The fear of the Lord gives us the courage to follow his sovereign commands, even when we do not understand the situation, and this is essential for good leadership.
- When we fear Abba, we have an unshakable and steadfast conviction that God is great and God is good. Because of these convictions, we will boldly and faithfully obey his commands. The world may view our actions as courageous, and indeed they are, but we also know that the safest place one can be is in the center of God's will and in that we find comfort.

POINTS TO PONDER

- Are there courageous steps God wants you to take? If so, what are they?

- How will the fear of the Lord help you take those actions? Be as specific as you can.

6

THE KEY TO EVANGELISM

Therefore, knowing the fear of the Lord, we persuade others.
2 Corinthians 5:11 ESV

"Then I praised the Most High; I honored and glorified him who lives forever."
Daniel 4:34

T here will be some wonderful surprises when we get to heaven, people we never expected to see at this last, great, family reunion. For example, the man who penned the second quotation above was a brutal tyrant who was able to conquer much of the known world. His authority was absolute, and anyone who opposed him or did not worship him was destroyed. He was also one of the world's greatest architects and built what is still considered one of the seven greatest wonders of the ancient world.

But through a series of miraculous events, God finally touched his heart and humbled him. This feared leader learned the fear of the Lord, acknowledged God as the Most High, and "honored and glorified him who lives forever." He then orchestrated what is still the single greatest

75

evangelism outreach this world has ever seen, for he wrote down his testimony, translated it into all the languages of all the people in his immense empire, and commanded that it be distributed and read to all his subjects. By his command, hundreds of millions of people heard about the Most High God for the first time ever. His testimony was distributed and read to people in all or parts of modern-day Egypt, Israel, Jordan, Lebanon, Syria, Iraq, Saudi Arabia, Turkey, Iran, Armenia, Kuwait, United Arab Emirates, Qatar, Georgia, Azerbaijan, Cyprus, and Russia.

Who was this man? None other than the Babylonian King Nebuchadnezzar. His written testimony describing the events leading to his conversion is recorded in Daniel, chapter four. Never before or since has the king or leader of such a vast empire had such a dramatic conversion experience and then provided a written testimony to all his subjects. But it took many years for God to get Nebuchadnezzar's attention.

It began with a dream so startling to Nebuchadnezzar that he had to be absolutely confident of its interpretation. So he commanded his court enchanters to tell him both the dream and its interpretation or face execution. When the executioners came to the prophet Daniel's house in Babylon to get him, Daniel asked for twenty-four hours of reprieve. He and his three friends, Shadrach, Meshach, and Abednego, prayed, and that night God revealed the dream and its interpretation to Daniel.

Upon revealing this to the king, Nebuchadnezzar praised the God of Daniel. He said, "Surely your God is the God of gods and the Lord of kings and a revealer of mysteries, for you were able to reveal this mystery."[143] But Nebuchadnezzar still saw the great Revealer as Daniel's God, not his.

Next, King Nebuchadnezzar built a huge golden image (perhaps of himself) ninety feet high and nine feet wide. He commanded all the leaders in his empire to attend the dedication. Once his Babylonian band started playing, everyone was commanded to bow down and worship the golden image. Despite the grave consequences of their actions, Daniel's three Hebrew friends, Shadrach, Meshach, and Abednego, stood their ground and refused to bow to this heathen god.[144] King Nebuchadnezzar was furious that these three had defied his direct order to worship the image, so he commanded that they be thrown into a blazing furnace heated so hot that it killed the soldiers who threw the three men into it. Shadrach, Meshach, and Abednego not only survived their punishment, but in the middle of the furnace, they received the protection of an angel who may have been the preincarnate Christ, the Son of God. They came out of the fire unharmed, with not even a hair on their heads burned.

King Nebuchadnezzar praised "the God of Shadrach, Meshach and Abednego, who has sent his angel and rescued his servants." But, once again, the king saw the ultimate Deliverer as the God of Shadrach, Meshach, and Abednego; it was not Nebuchadnezzar's God.

Then we come to the fourth chapter of the book of Daniel, which tells about King Nebuchadnezzar's written testimony sent "to the peoples, nations and men of every language, who live in all the world" (Daniel 4:1). The king says in verse 2, "It is my pleasure to tell you about the miraculous signs and wonders that the Most High God has performed for me." Here we see a subtle but critically important change in this pagan king. For him, God is no longer Daniel's God or Shadrach's God. The Lord is now Nebuchadnezzar's God, and he declares that God's wonders were performed "for me."

In his testimony, the king tells the story of another dream he had, also interpreted by Daniel, that warned him that unless he humbled himself and acknowledged that "the Most High is sovereign over the kingdoms of men and gives them to anyone he wishes" that he would be driven away from his people for seven years and live with the wild animals, eating grass like cattle. Despite this warning, Nebuchadnezzar refused to yield to God.

The king had built one of the greatest cities the world had ever seen. It is said that the walls of Babylon were 56 miles in length, 320 feet high, and 80 feet wide. One of the seven wonders of the world, the hanging gardens of Babylon which were part of Nebuchadnezzar's palace were a series of terraced gardens 400 feet square and rising 80 feet that contained every tree and plant in his kingdom. Water was pumped to the top where a sophisticated irrigation system watered all the various plants, shrubs, and trees.[145] "There were in it also several artificial rocks, that had the resemblance of mountains; with nurseries of all sorts of plants, and a kind of hanging garden suspended in the air by a most admirable contrivance. This was to gratify his wife, who, being brought up in Media, among the hills, and in the fresh air, found relief from such a prospect."[146]

Twelve months after his dream, King Nebuchadnezzar was walking on the roof of his palace when he boastfully said, "Is not this the great Babylon I have built as the royal residence, by my mighty power and for the glory of my majesty?" While the king's words were still "on his lips, a voice came from heaven, 'This is what is decreed for you, King Nebuchadnezzar: Your royal authority has been taken from you. You will be driven away from people and will live with the wild animals; you will eat grass like the ox. Seven times will pass by for you until you acknowledge that the Most High is sovereign over all kingdoms on earth and gives them to anyone he wishes.' " Immediately insanity struck King Nebuchadnezzar; he was driven away from his people; he lived outdoors, ate grass like cattle, and his hair and nails grew wild. [147]

In his testimony, King Nebuchadnezzar writes: "At the end of that time, I, Nebuchadnezzar, raised my eyes toward heaven, and my sanity was restored. Then I praised the Most High; I honored and glorified him who lives forever."[148] Sanity restored, he assumed his throne and his kingdom became greater than before. The king concludes with these sobering words about God: "everything he does is right and all his ways are just. And those who walk in pride he is able to humble."[149] The mighty king had been humbled and had had a true fear-of-the-Lord experience. As a result, hundreds of millions of souls heard about the Most High, the God of heaven who is just and mighty, whose supreme "kingdom endures from generation to generation."[150]

As Nebuchadnezzar discovered, the fear of Abba instills in us a holy compulsion to share with others the marvelous story of the grace that we have been given; the story is just too good to keep it to ourselves. Why did such a mighty God set his affection on little ol' me and then send his only Son to redeem me from my sin? Why did the Creator of a billion galaxies, who can do anything he pleases, choose the bloody path of redemption rather than just wiping the slate clean and starting over with a new, sinless creation? For anyone captivated by the fear of Abba, these persistent questions remain unanswered and the only remaining, compelling response is one of praise and gratitude for this merciful God—a response we cannot hide but must be shared. We hunger for others to join us in the celebration of this Holy Abba who is to be feared simply because of his inexplicable love.

Lessons from a Thief

"Salvation is near those who fear him [God]."[151]

Jesus did not die alone. The Romans saw fit to place two criminals, one on either side of him, at Golgotha.

One of the criminals who hung there hurled insults at him: "Aren't you the Messiah? Save yourself and us!"

But the other criminal rebuked him, "Don't you fear God," he said, "since you are under the same sentence? We are punished justly, for we are getting what our deeds deserve. But this man has done nothing wrong."

Then he said, "Jesus, remember me when you come into your kingdom."

Jesus answered him, "Truly I tell you, today you will be with me in paradise."[152]

What a contrast! Two criminals. The first was spiteful, angry, hateful, and cursing. He was mad at the Roman criminal justice system that was now executing him. He was scheming to the bitter end by hurling insults and taunts at Jesus to entice him to use his magical powers to "spring" all three of them.

The other criminal acknowledged his guilt; he admitted that his crimes were deserving of death. He realized that the grace and mercy he saw in Jesus were in stark contrast to his own life. He had already heard Jesus say those incredible words as he hung on the cross, "Father, forgive them, for they do not know what they are doing."[153] He had marveled at what kind of man could say such things. He recognized that of the three of them undergoing crucifixion, it was Jesus who was being treated unjustly.

Two criminals.

Suffering for the same crime.

Receiving the same punishment.

But each had different reactions to the man who hung between them.

Why? Because one of them feared God and the other did not. "Don't you fear God," the one said as he rebuked his fellow criminal. "We are punished justly, for we are getting what our deeds deserve. But this man has done nothing wrong."

Although both had chosen to live a life of crime, one had been taught, probably early in his life, right from wrong, good from evil, and had been forewarned of the consequences of sinful actions. One had probably been raised by God-fearing parents who instilled in him as a child a fear of Abba and taught him that God was a God of justice and mercy. Both men had engaged in criminal activities, but on the cross, one remembered what he had been taught years before, humbled himself, and admitted his guilt. He did not ask Jesus to forgive him; he could only bring himself to ask Jesus to remember him when he came into his kingdom. But Jesus saw his humility, forgave him, and granted him eternal salvation.

Redeeming Fear

On October 4, 1988, televangelist Jim Bakker was indicted on charges of mail fraud, wire fraud, and defrauding the public and sentenced to forty-five years in prison. In 1980, he had a sexual encounter with his secretary, Jessica Hahn, and then he tried to cover-up his liaison by paying her $350,000—funds that were not his to give. Although his sentence was later reduced to eight years, his conviction and sentencing collapsed his long-time ministry and his 2,200-acre theme park, Heritage USA, that two years earlier had attracted six million visitors, second only to the Disney theme parks.

Christian author John Bevere visited Jim Bakker in the federal prison in Rochester, Minnesota. The now humble and repentant Bakker offered this very insightful comment as he reflected back on what had happened and the genesis of his tragic situation: "John, I never stopped loving God; I stopped fearing God."[154] Jim Bakker joined the thief on the cross when he realized that had he feared God, he would not have committed his sinful and criminal actions.

Three times in Scripture we are told, "God opposes the proud but gives grace to the humble."[155] Like King Nebuchadnezzar found after seven humbling years, the fear of the Lord creates humility in us; it cannot coexist with human pride.

When we fear God, we possess an awesome reverence for his greatness, and we realize that his incredible power and love stand in sharp contrast to our lives.

When we fear God, we can't help but wonder why a God with such power would also have such mercy on us.

When we fear Abba, we realize, like the thief on the cross, that our sins also deserve eternal damnation, which leads us to marvel at his mercy and be puzzled by his grace.

Our natural inclination is then to share with others this newly found story of personal redemption, knowing that the whys will remain unanswered, even in eternity, and that's okay.

> But in your hearts *revere* Christ as Lord. Always be prepared to give
> an answer to everyone who asks you to give the reason for the hope
> that you have. But do this *with gentleness and respect.*[156]

When we fear and love Abba, his love for the lost becomes imprinted on our hearts, and we gladly join him in the pursuit of *his* lost sheep, for "the earth is the LORD's and everything in it, the world, and all who live in it."[157] We are not content for those lost sheep to happen to stumble across the safety of the sheep pen and the protection of the shepherd. No, they must be sought out through well-planned search and rescue operations that find the lost sheep wherever they are, in whatever shape they are in, to entice them to do as we have done—to willingly join the flock of the Good Shepherd where there is abundant safety and provision.

Like someone who has just received wonderful news, news that cannot be stilled, our obsessive joy is to be the one who reintroduces them to their Creator, to bring them home to the place they have never been before where their soul finds the rest it has longed for and their spirit comes alive with the Holy Spirit who first hovered over the waters of creation and gave them their breath of life. We desperately want his ways and salvation to be known upon the earth and "among all nations … so that all the ends of the earth will fear him."[158] We now know that the fear of Abba is not something to be afraid of. Rather, it is the inevitable outcome of finally comprehending, as best we can, God's overwhelming and inexplicable mercy and love for us—that love that latches on to us and stubbornly refuses to let us go.

"So that all the ends of the earth will fear him," the psalmist says.[159] The fear of Abba is God's grand finale and ultimate purpose.

"Therefore, knowing the fear of the Lord, we persuade others"[160] with the good news, the gospel of Jesus Christ.

> Then I saw another angel flying in midair, and he had the *eternal* gospel to proclaim to those who live on the earth—to every nation, tribe, language and people. He said in a loud voice, "*Fear God and give him glory*, because the hour of his judgment has come. Worship him who made the heavens, the earth, the sea and the springs of water."[161]

According to the book of Revelation, and like King Nebuchadnezzar discovered, the gospel, God's good news to all people, must include the fear of God, and it is incomplete without it. For evangelism to be effective, we must proclaim the *eternal* gospel of Jesus Christ—an everlasting truth that transcends time itself—and it must include two elements: the fear of God and the worship of our Creator-King.

 POINTS TO PERSONALIZE

- We need not be afraid of fearing God for it is the natural result of us understanding, as best we can, his inexplicable love for us and his incredible power.
- As we grow in our fear of the Lord, our love for those who have not yet found Christ will also grow, and we will feel compelled to share our story of how the Good Shepherd found us.

 POINTS TO PONDER

- What lost sheep has God placed on your heart?

- What well-planned search and rescue operation can you be part of to reach them?

7

THE WISE BUILDER

Many of us are familiar with Jesus's parable of the wise man who built his house upon the rock, and the foolish man who built his house upon the sand. The rains came down, the streams rose, and the wind blew. The house built on the rock stood fast, while the other fell with a great crash. The conclusion that most draw from the story, and the conclusion of the familiar Sunday school song, is to build our lives on the "rock," the Lord Jesus Christ. But that rather vague idea is not the point that Jesus was making in this parable. Let's take a second look.

> "Therefore, everyone who hears these words of mine and puts them into practice is like a wise man who built his house on the rock. The rain came down, the streams rose, and the winds blew and beat against that house; yet it did not fall, because it had its foundation on the rock. But everyone who hears these words of mine and does not put them into practice is like a foolish man who built his house on sand. The rain came down, the streams rose, and the winds blew and beat against that house, and it fell with a great crash."[162]

The parable contains an interesting parallel construction. Both men designed their own homes and obtained the necessary building materials. Both spent months constructing the floors, the walls, the roof, roughing it in, adding windows and doors and roofing material, finishing the interior, and completing all the other endless tasks associated with building a home. To the casual observer, both houses were well-constructed homes. Then, both homes encountered a terribly strong storm with rain, rising water, and dangerous wind. The final outcome is where the parallelism ends. One home stood firm because it was built on a secure foundation; the other was destroyed.

Then Jesus draws his conclusion: "Therefore, everyone who hears these words of mine *and puts them into practice* …." In the parable, both men heard Jesus's words. One of them chose to put these words into practice, and one did not. One man intentionally applied the words that Jesus spoke to his daily life; one ignored them. One man purposefully changed his ways as a result; one disregarded what Jesus said and went his own way instead. The wise man obeyed Jesus's teachings, thus creating a firm foundation; the foolish man disobeyed them and built a home that lacked the most important element of all—a solid foundation.

The single point in the parable was to teach the importance of obedience to Jesus's instructions and to graphically illustrate the complete destruction that follows disobedience. A person cannot easily fix a flawed foundation and certainly not in the midst of a storm. In the middle of this ferocious storm, the home the foolish man built, that was intended to provide shelter from the elements, collapsed, exposing the man and his family to incredible danger.

It is hard to overstate the importance of a foundation, and yet it is hidden and buried in the ground, unseen by anyone. The foundation determines the width, length, height, and weight of the house, and every portion of the home must eventually find its support in the foundation that then transfers the weight of the structure to the immovable soil or bedrock of the earth. If the foundation is flawed, the house will shift, walls will crack, plumbing may break, windows and doors will not open or close, and eventually all will be lost.

But the foolish man thought that he had built a solid home that was secure. In fact, he thought that he had found a new, cost-saving way to build houses. He believed that he had discovered, because of his own ingenuity, a clever way to avoid sinking money and effort into a foundation, something that no one sees, and instead put that money to use where it really mattered. He deceived himself into thinking that he could skip the time and expense of building a foundation and moved immediately to building the flashy, exciting parts of the house. He willingly entered into deception and foolishly thought he could dispense with the foundation.

Jesus's parable was told to call his hearers to build their lives on his teachings; these are the firm foundation on which to erect and direct our lives. We cannot simply attend Jesus's church and call that good enough. We must apply his teachings to our lives. The apostle James (Jesus's brother) said, "Do not merely listen to the word, and so deceive yourselves. Do what it says."[163] In fact, hearing the Word of God and not acting on it puts us in a more dangerous situation than never hearing it in the first place, for those who merely listen to God's Word deceive themselves into thinking that obedient actions are not needed, that the house of their life can be built without the foundation of God's truth applied. They enter into a false sense of security and believe that their spiritual foundation is strong and able to withstand the trials of this life and the attacks of satan. They do not believe that they are living on shifting sand and that the next storm will bring down their life. Attending church, participating in worship, joining a small group, praying, reading the Bible, listening to Christian radio, and even meditating on the Word of God do not, in themselves, create a firm foundation if God's Word is not applied to our lives and our hearts changed. That is the not-so-subtle point that Jesus is making in this parable.

Jesus said that after hearing his words, they must be put into practice. Nothing else can substitute for true, heartfelt, and joyful obedience to God's Word. In other words, we must choose to allow the eternal, powerful, living, active, and energetic Word of God[164] to marvelously reveal our inner self, to penetrate the inmost recesses of our heart, to judge our motives, to mold our lives, to awaken our conscience, and to craft our character. The Bible, according to the late journalist Malcolm Muggeridge, is "the book that reads me," and we must be reformed by it.

When evangelist John Wesley (1703–1791) was returning home from a service one night, he was robbed. The thief, however, found his victim to have only a little money and some Christian literature. As the bandit was leaving, Wesley called out, "Stop, I have something more to give you." The surprised robber paused. "My friend," said Wesley, "you may live to regret this sort of life. If you ever do, here's something to remember: 'The blood of Jesus Christ cleanses us from all sin!' " The thief hurried away, and Wesley prayed that his words might bear fruit.

Years later, Wesley was greeting people after a Sunday service when he was approached by a stranger. What a surprise to learn that this visitor, now a believer in Christ as a successful businessman, was the one who had robbed him years before! "I owe it all to you," said the transformed man. "Oh no, my friend," Wesley exclaimed, "not to me, but to the precious blood of Christ that cleanses us from all sin!"[165]

The applied Word of God transforms our lives, but foundations take time to build. Ideally, foundations begin early in life as a child learns to quickly obey his parents. Sometimes the child understands the logic behind the instruction to obey, and sometimes he must act out of sheer obedience without understanding the whys. And so it is in our relationship with God. He tells us that "As the heavens are higher than the earth, so are my ways higher than your ways and my thoughts than your thoughts."[166] The foundation of obedience that begins in childhood serves one purpose—to teach us to obey a God who sometimes explains himself and sometimes asks us to obey commands that are hard and may make no sense to us, like loving our enemies.

"You have heard that it was said, 'You shall love your neighbor and hate your enemy.' But I say to you, Love your enemies and pray for those who persecute you, so that you may be sons of your Father who is in heaven." (Matthew 5:43–45 ESV)

Who is an "enemy"? When Jesus said this, I am sure the crowd immediately thought of the Roman soldiers occupying their land and their many atrocities. When we read this, we may think of those forces in the world, such as communism and radical Islam, that are intent on destroying freedom throughout the world. Or we may think of political adversaries on the other side of the aisle, or neighbors down the street who seem more intent on irritating us than getting along with us.

But what if it is more personal than that?

What if that "enemy" is your business competitor? Are we to extend blessings even to those with whom we compete? Is that carrying this concept a bit too far? These were some of the questions that raced through my mind more than thirty years ago. Can one own and run a business in such a way that it blesses God *and* my competitors?

I didn't pursue my MBA at the University of Denver thinking that my wife and I would one day be entrepreneurs and own a consulting and administration business. Yet I sat in my office on Monday, August 1st, 1988 having just bought Retirement Planning Services, a fledgling two-person company. I knew the clients and they knew me because I had already worked in the company for two years after receiving my MBA in 1986. Strangely, however, very little of my MBA training had prepared me to own a business. I had studied the recently deregulated airline industry, calculated bond prices when interest rates rise and fall, examined the elasticity of demand of different types of goods and services, was adept at future value and present value calculations, and could build and design database structures, but no one had trained me on how to run a payroll, remit tax withholdings, manage cash flow, and create a marketing plan with no marketing budget. My wife and I had discussed at length the crazy idea of purchasing this business and concluded that God was definitely leading us to do that. We both felt that this company was an incredible gift to us from God, given for us to grow and develop with him as our unseen business partner, our chairman of the board. Who can turn down an opportunity to go into business with God?

We literally believe that we have an unseen business partner. God is not some imaginary friend such as our daughter had as a child; he's real. Through my faith in Jesus Christ as my Lord and Savior, I have another family with God as my Father. He is just as involved and interested in what I do Monday through Saturday as what I do on Sunday. Not only does he love me far more than even my loving, earthly father does, but he is also all-knowing and all-powerful. If you're looking for the best candidate for a CEO position, I think God qualifies. Who better to have in charge of strategic planning, marketing, and employee recruitment than the One who created us and this universe, knows what will happen today, tomorrow, and ten years from now, and wants us to succeed (using his definition of success) even more than we do?

It would take years for me to develop the fear-of-the-Lord concepts that I have laid out in this book, but my wife and I knew even then that God blesses obedience and that, like the wise man in the parable, if this business was to have a sure foundation, we needed to hear the Word of God and put it into practice.

The year 2020 marks the thirty-second year of owning our business and the thirty-second consecutive year of business growth. Even during the storm of the recent Great Recession, we grew and even doubled in size. My unseen business partner is amazing and has led and guided this business in some incredible ways. Here is one story.

In the fall of 2015, after reading Verne Harnish's book *Scaling Up*, my management team came to me and asked why we have an office. Why can't people just work from home? Why do they need to spend hours fighting Denver traffic? I must admit that I initially thought the idea was nuts. How can you create a great company culture with a remote workforce? How do you introduce new employees to the business, including the existing staff and culture, and train them? But I've learned that my unseen business partner often speaks through others and I must listen. Our office lease was up September 30, 2017, so we had twenty-one months to analyze, prepare, and test possible options. My managers code-named the project Gypsy.

We experimented for twenty months. We sent the staff out for two days, three days, then one to two weeks. They returned and told us what worked and what didn't. Although we had done all this preliminary work, I knew that transitioning to a remote environment would be the greatest challenge the company had ever faced because everything would have to change, including our computer system and IT structure, how we manage, how we do reviews, how we monitor workflow, and how we hire. But I pulled the trigger and transitioned the staff to a remote workforce the spring and summer of 2017.

On September 1st of 2017, I was still wrestling with the decision we had made to deploy all our staff into a remote environment. As I drove east on Belleview Avenue close to the prior office, I prayed, "Lord, you've got to help me out here. Was it a mistake to implement Gypsy?" At that moment, I looked up and read the license plate of the car directly in front of me. I quickly got out my phone and snapped this picture.

I think God has quite the sense of humor, don't you? If you doubt that there is a God and that he wants to be a part of our everyday life, consider the odds of seeing this car directly in front of me at that precise moment of time. I had never seen this vehicle before and have never seen it since.

Also, notice that the car is a Honda Pilot. As a part of the Gypsy project, and as recommended in Verne Harnish's wonderful book *Scaling Up*, in 2016 my management team had developed a set of core company values that define the company's DNA: PILOT. God doesn't miss much; apparently, he likes our values statements too.

```
LIVES WITH PURPOSE
                IMPROVES THE EXPERIENCE
COMMITTED TO LEARNING
                OWNS THE RESULTS
BELIEVES IN THE TEAM
```

Going remote has proven to be one of the most important strategic decisions this company has ever made. During the COVID-19 pandemic of 2020, while other businesses were scrambling to deploy their employees into a remote work environment, we continued to operate as we had for the prior three years in a secure, well-functioning remote office structure, and we continued to grow.

And yes, we continue to bless our competitors by praying for them, helping them, sharing with them ideas that we have found to be successful, and even referring business to them when appropriate.

This is just one of many examples of how obedience to the Word of God always brings about his blessings in our lives in the manner that he sees fit.

Perhaps your spiritual foundation is shaky, and you struggle with obeying and putting into practice Jesus's teachings. Perhaps you were not raised in a home where godly obedience was taught in a loving and gentle way. Or perhaps your parents did attempt to teach you godly obedience, but you rebelled against their authority and now you have a difficult time obeying God, an authority figure you cannot see. There's still time for you to shift your foundation to one that's solid and help you stand no matter what this life throws at you.

The Fear of Abba Is the Pathway of Obedience

Isaac had been born to Abraham and Sarah when Abraham was a hundred years old and Sarah was ninety-one. Fifteen years later, while living in southern Israel at a place Abraham named Beersheba, God again spoke to Abraham.

> Some time later God tested Abraham. He said to him, "Abraham!"
>
> "Here I am," he replied.
>
> Then God said, "Take your son, your only son, whom you love—Isaac—and go to the region of Moriah. Sacrifice him there as a burnt offering on a mountain I will show you."[167]

So Abraham and Isaac traveled by foot from Beersheba to Mount Moriah, about fifty-five miles. In obedience, Abraham prepared an altar, placed wood on it, and bound Isaac and put him on the altar. As he was getting ready to slay his son, an angel appeared and said:

> "Do not lay a hand on the boy," he said. "Do not do anything to him. Now I know that you fear God, because you have not withheld from me your son, your only son."[168]

Notice that the angel did not say, "Now I know that you will obey God." Instead he said, "Now I know that you fear God." God is more concerned that we fear him than obey him, for one who truly fears the Lord will always obey him. The proper fear of Abba is a fail-safe way to submit to him, for someone who fears the Lord always acts on his instructions. The fear of the Lord, instilled in us through the power of the Holy Spirit, is at the root of true and continuous obedience.

Remember, the fear of the Lord can only be properly understood within the context of family. When we properly fear our heavenly Father, we know that he will discipline us for unconfessed sin and rebellion, but we also know that our chastisement is for our good.[169] When we fear Abba, we gladly accept his loving authority. Our obedience, then, is a natural result.

It is easy to obey God when we agree with his command, when we see the merit of his instruction and the wisdom of his directive. However, it is far more difficult to obey God when his instructions are counterintuitive and defy human understanding, as they often do. At such times the fear of the Lord will remind us of God's admonition in Isaiah: "As the heavens are higher than the earth, so are my ways higher than your ways and my thoughts than your thoughts." Sometimes, understanding the ways of God is about as futile as explaining calculus to my cat.

The fear of the Lord reminds us of who we are and who God is, that he is omniscient and we are not, that God has no duty to us to justify or explain his actions but that is okay because, like the story I told of the police officer who is also our father, we know that God's actions emanate from his loving heart and therefore we implicitly trust him.

Where you see the reverence of the Lord, you will also find obedience to his Word. Notice this passage from Isaiah, "Who among you fears the LORD *and obeys* the word of his servant?" and from Ecclesiastes, "here is the conclusion of the matter: Fear God *and keep his commandments.*"[170] Having a fear and reverence for God are first, then obedience follows. Obedience is not such a struggle for those who fear and love God because obedience is a natural response.

Recall that in Exodus 20, Moses brought the children of Israel to the foot of Mount Sinai to meet with God and have him speak the Ten Commandments to them. They saw the lightening, heard the thunder and the blast of a trumpet, and felt the earth shake beneath them. It was a terribly frightening experience to come that close to the Lord and hear him speak, so much so that the people told Moses, "Speak to us yourself and we will listen. But do not have God speak to us or we will die." Moses replied with a very insightful admonition: "Do not be afraid. God has come to test you, so that the fear of God will be with you to keep you from sinning."[171] Once again, the fear of God and obedience to his Word go hand in hand, but fear comes first.

The evidence of the fear of God, or lack thereof, came at the conclusion of a test, as it always does. Abraham passed his test. The children of Israel failed theirs, for it was not but forty days later, after Moses had gone up to the top of Mount Sinai to meet with God a second time but had not yet returned, that they reverted to idolatry and made and worshiped the blasphemous golden calf. The children of Israel disobeyed God when they did not fear him. God then disciplined them, which led to their temporary repentance and obedience, only to have the cycle repeat itself—over and over again.

Abraham had every human reason not to obey God. The command for him to sacrifice the son God had promised him made no sense at all. Wasn't Isaac the one who was to bless all the nations of the earth? Weren't the descendants of Isaac to be as numerous as the sands of the sea? Yet God had specifically spoken to Abraham, of that he was sure, and his command to kill Isaac was not to be ignored, challenged, or defied.

Abraham knew that at his core God was very good. Yes, God was great, awesome, sovereign, and someone to be feared, but he was also loving and someone to be trusted. God's character was not capricious, of this he was sure. Abraham would have agreed with what King David later wrote: "Let those who fear the LORD say: 'His love endures forever.' "[172] The fear of Abba and the love of Abba are joined together. Therefore, Abraham had to conclude that this very strange and counterintuitive command of God was reasonable, loving, and well-intended because it would have been inconsistent with God's character for him to act in any other way. He trusted God's love for him, even while fearing his great power, and he embraced this seeming paradox.

So Abraham bravely obeyed God. It was pure, determined obedience, and God had no Plan B. Abraham did not even bring a lamb with him. He knew that any other sacrifice, while pleasing to God at other times, would have been an act of disobedience. He did not want to rationalize any other form of sacrifice and so he intentionally left himself no alternative.

The angel responded by saying, "Now I know that you fear God." The Hebrew word used here for "know" is *yada*. It conveys a covenantal knowing, a deep intimacy, a profound core conviction in someone. In Scripture, *yada* is often used to describe the knowing between a husband and a wife: "Adam knew [*yada*] Eve."[173] Elsewhere the term describes a covenantal knowing or understanding of someone. When King David writes, "Search me, O God, and know my heart; try me and know my anxious thoughts,"[174] he is using the word *yada*. By using this word, the angel in effect says to Abraham, "Now I know that I know that I know that you deeply and reverentially fear God while also trusting his character and embracing his infinite love for you."

It is no wonder, then, that King David also wrote, "Who, then, are those who fear the LORD? He will instruct them in the ways they should choose."[175] Rather than frantically seeking out God's will in our lives, we should instead focus on developing a profound fear of the Lord in our hearts for the psalmist says that God's will is revealed to those who fear God.

If you have ever sailed or watched a sailing boat, you understand that the positioning of the sails and the rudder determine the direction of the craft; the wind doesn't set the boat's direction. When we choose to fear Abba, through the power of the Holy Spirit, we also choose to obey him, thus setting our sails and charting our course to follow him. The proper fear of Abba, instilled in us through the Holy Spirit, becomes our spiritual GPS system that guides and directs our lives. Winds of adversity that blow other ships off course and away from God only propel us faster along God's pathway because we have chosen to revere a loving, heavenly Father who we know is truly kind and compassionate and only wants his best for us. God is great, *and* God is good. We can trust a God like that.

One ship sails East,
And another West,
By the self-same winds that blow,
'Tis the set of the sails
And not the gales,
That tells the way we go.[176]

 POINTS TO PERSONALIZE

- Only hearing the word of God and not obeying it creates in us a false sense of security since we do not realize that only obedience to God's Word gives us a strong foundation that will withstand the storms of this life.
- Storms are inevitable, but a weak foundation is not, and rebuilding a foundation in the midst of a storm is quite difficult!
- The fear of the Lord is central to a true and continuous obedience to God, which then creates in us the strong foundation.

 POINTS TO PONDER

- Identify an issue in your life that you struggle with. Can you trace that issue back to sin? If so, can you trace it back one step further to a lack of the fear of God? Explain your answers.

- Would this sin have happened had you instead obeyed God because you feared him? Write down your thoughts and ask God to forgive your sin and move forward with him in obedience to his Word.

- Are you in the midst of a storm of life? How has your prior obedience to God formed your foundation?

- Or, has this storm of life shaken your spiritual house? If so, ask the Holy Spirit to reveal to you steps of obedience that you need to take.

8

RECEIVING THE FEAR OF ABBA

As we've seen so far, the fear of Abba is not something to be afraid of but rather is a precious gift of love from the Giver of gifts and is only for our good, for it keeps us from sin and all of sin's devastation. It calibrates our spiritual GPS system as we mature in our faith and "work out [our] salvation with fear and trembling."[177] The only antidote to the snare that is the fear of man[178] is the fear of the Lord for the two fears can never coexist. Although all of us will encounter the inevitable spiritual storms of life, we will not be destroyed by these storms if we have already built our spiritual house on a firm foundation, created through hearing *and obeying* the Word of God. At the root of true and continuous obedience is the fear of the Lord. If our goal is to be like Christ, then we must, like him, take great delight in the fear of Abba, knowing that our prayers, like Jesus's, are heard because of our reverent submission. Along with these truths, we've learned that the fear of Abba is indispensable to fulfilling the Great Commission, for it instills in us a holy compulsion to share with others the marvelous story of the grace that we have been given; the story is just too good to keep it to ourselves.

Granting all of these things, how do we develop a proper reverence and fear of Abba? We need to begin by meditating on the undeserved grace and forgiveness that we have already received from God.

> Out of the depths I cry to you, O Lord!
>> O Lord, hear my voice!
> Let your ears be attentive
>> to the voice of my pleas for mercy!
> If you, O Lord, should mark iniquities,
>> O Lord, who could stand?
> *But with you there is forgiveness,*
>> *that you may be feared.*[179]

Contemplating the mysterious love of God sows the seeds from which spring a deep and profound gratitude that he has abstained from marking my iniquities and from keeping an unabridged black book of all the sins I have committed. In fact, he has buried them in the deepest sea and put up a "No fishing" sign. I may remember my sins, but God has chosen to forget them, and he has chosen to adopt me into his forever family. The apostle Paul reminds us, "In him we have redemption through his blood, the forgiveness of sins, in accordance with the riches of God's grace that he lavished on us."[180] God's forgiveness of us flows out of his superabundant grace.

For several years I worked in the Admissions Office of a university, and one of my jobs was to interview prospective students. I conducted hundreds of interviews, but one is etched into my memory. One fall day, Billie K. and his father sat down in my office, and after exchanging the customary introductions, Billie's father explained to me that Billie had been chosen. I thought he was being rather presumptuous since I had not yet admitted Billie to the university, although he certainly had the grades and background for which we were looking. Seeing my confusion, Billie's father explained that most parents are not granted the opportunity that they had been given to choose their own children. Then I understood. Billie had been adopted into their family, and this proud father, who was grinning from ear to ear, could not have been more delighted and pleased with his son.

When I contemplate the love of God, I often think of Billie's father, for we, too, have been adopted into God's family. Abba chose us, loves us, and has forgiven us. The eternal why for his actions may never be answered. But we can rest assured, as the apostle John wrote, that we can "see what great love the Father has lavished on us, that we should be called children of God!"[181]

God could have chosen to do something differently. He could have rejected the human race that had rejected him, abandoned his redemptive plan and started over, and left us destined for hell and eternal separation from him. Considering God's alternative options and the grace he has given to us should nurture in our lives the fear of the Lord. That is why the psalmist wrote, "But with you there is forgiveness, that you may be feared."[182]

As we discovered in chapter one, the proper fear of Abba is also a quest. We must search for it as if it were hidden treasure. We are not born with it; it is not an instinctual fear like animals have with their fear of man. No, it must be taught. King David wrote, "Come, my children, listen to me; I will teach you the fear of the LORD."[183] The fear of Abba is a quest, but it is a guided quest, and ideally, it is taught by parents to their children, or at least by spiritual parents to their spiritual children. It is a wonderful spiritual heritage, handed down from generation to generation that is full of lifelong blessings.

King David prayed, "Teach me your way, LORD, that I may rely on your faithfulness; give me an undivided heart, that I may fear your name."[184] He asked to be taught and willingly became a student, then he began by acknowledging that the ways of the Lord, God's truth, an undivided heart, and the fear of the Lord are all wonderous gifts sent from God. King David knew that the natural inclination of our sinful hearts is to run and hide from God, just as Adam and Eve did after their initial sin, and that only the kindness of God draws us to him. The magnetic strength of the Holy Spirit enraptures us and gently nudges us to follow the paths of God while still giving us a free will to choose his way and his truth.

Years ago, my son and I took beginning snowboarding lessons on the beautiful slopes of Keystone Ski Resort in Colorado. The instructor told us that we could steer our boards by just looking in the direction we wanted to go. To my surprise, such a subtle change shifted the weight on the board and sent it in the direction I was looking.

As Christians, we sometimes work and strive too hard when all we must do to change the direction of our lives is to "[look] to Jesus, the founder and perfecter of our faith."[185] He not only gives us the faith to believe in him, but through the power of the Holy Spirit, he is also perfecting it, changing us, and sanctifying us. But we must do something—choose to look to Jesus. Like King David, we must choose to ask God to teach us his way so that we can walk in his truth and to give us a heart with one pure and holy passion whose single mission is to fear and love God. We should pray: *Lord, what divides my heart? What causes me to not be wholly devoted to you? Have I engaged in idolatry by worshiping something or someone other than you, such as my career, prestige, or money?*

When we hear the term *idol*, we often think of physical, metal, or wooden objects that have been formed to represent some deity that is worshiped, such as Buddha or a Hindu god, and we may think that the lack of any physical idols in our homes means we are free of idolatry. However, an idol is anything in our life that is more important than God. We can refer to these as "soft idols." Physical idols are easy to spot. On the other hand, soft idols are very personal, hidden, and sneaky, are easily justified, and often masquerade as being good and wholesome. They are sometimes difficult to discern because they often appear to be so noble.

Who can fault someone who is outgoing and charming? Yet, if the applause of man is more important than the approval of God, this person has a divided heart, an idol.

Who can criticize an individual who plans out each day, week, and month with precision, accomplishing so much that people sit back and marvel at his or her productivity? Yet, if the esteem of others and the persona of success hold a greater attraction than the serenity of time spent with loved ones, with our Lord, and in rest, this person has a divided heart, an idol.

Who can fault parents who pour time and effort into making sure their kids have the best education and coaching so that they can excel in competitions, achieve near-perfect college entrance test scores, and earn scholarships to attend the best colleges that will launch their promising careers? Yet, if the parents have made their children, not God, the prime focus of their love and attention, they have a divided heart, an idol that bears a striking resemblance to their own kids! Our role as parents is not to help our children fulfill their personal dreams and aspirations, but to help them discover the fulfilling life God planned for them before they were even conceived: "Your eyes saw my unformed body; all the days ordained for me were written in your book before one of them came to be."[186]

What Is My "Golden Calf"?

Jesus warned us about having a divided heart when he said, "No one can serve two masters. Either you will hate the one and love the other, or you will be devoted to the one and despise the other. You cannot serve both God and money."[187] The love of money is a common heart-divider, will stunt our fear of Abba, and is the "root of all kinds of evil."[188]

But how do we know when we are serving money and not God? How do I know when money is my master and not God? When we serve money, it demands more and more of our time and attention and other things become subservient to it, for money's demands are insatiable and cannot be quenched. Does money drive your behavior and habits? Are you battling credit card debt? Do you find you never have enough money to tithe ten percent to the Lord? When we serve money, it will demand compromises of us that are at first seemingly trivial but become ever more serious. Perhaps it begins with not returning to the grocery store the excess change one mistakenly received and ends with stealing money from missionary retirement accounts through an illegal Ponzi scheme, such as what happened to a childhood friend of mine. When we love and serve money, we will choose a lifestyle that we cannot sustain without making compromises. We will work extra hours and weekends or take on a second job so that we can buy things we cannot afford with money we do not have to impress people we do not know.

Am I known for my generosity or my frugality (or both)? Do I follow Christ's example and kindly and freely give to those in need and feel the joy of the Lord well up within me when doing so?

We must ask ourselves, *Do we own our possessions, or is everything that we have a gift from God and we are only stewards of his generosity?* When we give to the Lord's work, do we have the attitude that we are only returning to him what he already owns and has so graciously given us?

Several years ago, in preparation for my son's wedding, I reserved a block of rooms at a local hotel. I did not know how many of the rooms would be used, but I knew that if I cancelled the room reservations three days ahead of time, I would not be charged for them. In the hectic pace of the wedding, I forgot to cancel the unused reservations, and I was charged for the rooms. My appeal to the hotel was of no avail. But I had a rather nonchalant attitude. "I tried, I forgot, oh well, nothing I can do about it now." And then the Holy Spirit impressed upon my heart, "That wasn't your money to waste!" Ouch! Am I a steward of God's gifts to me, or do I "own" my time, my money, and my possessions?

A few years ago, we discovered that a vehicle a good friend of ours owned was in very bad shape. My wife and I owned a nice, well-maintained Chevy Suburban that we were about to trade in for another vehicle. The Lord impressed upon our hearts to give our friend this vehicle, so I called him, told him what we wanted to do, and made arrangements for him to pick up the truck. In preparation, we had the vehicle serviced, all four tires replaced, filled it with gas, and cleaned it inside and out. And then we waited. My assumed appointment time came and went. Three hours later he arrived at our house. On the way to meeting us, he had stopped to climb a mountain with a friend, had underestimated the time it would take to safely climb it, did not have cell service to alert us, and did not recall setting a specific meeting time. Unaware of all this, by the time he arrived, I was a little annoyed, and the initial joy of giving was unfortunately gone.

However, I am so thankful for the misunderstanding because through it the Lord taught me an important lesson. Later, the Holy Spirit admonished me that I was a steward of the truck and not the owner, regardless of what the vehicle title stated, and I had no reason to be offended. My friend had innocently stopped to enjoy a smidgen of God's beautiful creation, and God was okay with that. By the way, as of this writing, that vehicle is still blessing this family and now has over 360,000 miles on it!

The psalmist asks God, "Give me an undivided heart, that I may fear your name." Fearing Abba is such an incredible gift from God, but it is not possible with a divided heart. Like the wise man who built his house upon the rock, we must choose to act upon the instructions Jesus gives us. We must be wholly devoted to him: "And whatever you do, whether in word or deed, do it all in the name of the Lord Jesus."[189] There should be no difference in how we act on Sunday versus Monday. Consistency of thought and action, word and deed—this is the mark of an undivided heart.

To underscore the importance of an undivided heart, Jesus said, "Love the LORD your God with *all* your heart and with *all* your soul and with *all* your mind and with *all* your strength."[190] Heart, soul, mind, and strength—nothing about us is untouched by his command.

Unity of heart and action is a decision we make, but it is also a gift from God. Speaking of the blessings of the new covenant, God through the prophet Jeremiah said:

> "They will be my people, and I will be their God. I will give them *singleness of heart and action, so that they will always fear me* and that all will then go well for them and for their children after them. I will make an everlasting covenant with them: I will never stop doing good to them, and I will inspire them to fear me, so that they will never turn away from me."[191]

The fear of Abba is a multigenerational gift from God, inspired by his love; it is an ongoing, eternal promise filled with God's goodness. But like salvation, it is a gift we must choose to receive, and receive it we must, for it alone will prevent us from turning away from God and rejecting him (as we discovered in chapter three).

God also provides the inspiration to fear him. This is found all around us, even in creation itself. Louis Pasteur, one of the founders of microbiology and a biologist renowned for his discoveries in the areas of vaccination and pasteurization, wrote, "The more I study nature, the more I stand amazed at the work of the Creator."[192]

King David wrote,

When I consider[193] your heavens,
    the work of your fingers,
the moon and the stars,
    which you have set in place,
what is mankind that you are mindful of them,
    human beings that you care for them?
You made them a little lower than the angels
    and crowned them with glory and honor.[194]

The careful and intentional study of God's creation, under the guidance of the Holy Spirit, inspired King David to fear Abba. After pondering over and over the work of God's fingers, the moon and stars, the startling greatness of God stunned him, the comparative weakness of man alarmed him, and the caring love of God overwhelmed him. That is the complete, well-rounded, mature fear of Abba initially revealed through a creation so vast that its size is incomprehensible, just like its Creator. Pondering God's creation is his common teaching method for instilling the fear of the Lord in us. As the psalmist wrote:

By the word of the LORD the heavens were made,
>   their starry host by the breath of his mouth.
He gathers the waters of the sea into jars,
>   he puts the deep into storehouses.
Let all the earth fear the LORD;
>   let all the people of the world revere him.
For he spoke, and it came to be;
>   he commanded, and it stood firm.[195]

The best tools to begin to develop a fear of Abba just might be a microscope and telescope. When trying to comprehend the greatness of God, there is no better illustration than creation, and that is where the writers of Scripture so frequently turn.

"To whom will you compare me?
>   Or who is my equal?" says the Holy One.
Lift up your eyes and look to the heavens:
>   Who created all these?
He who brings out the starry host one by one
>   and calls forth each of them by name.
Because of his great power and mighty strength,
>   not one of them is missing.[196]

We tend to view God's creation in scientific terms of neutrons, protons, cells, DNA, black holes, and light years, while forgetting the God who made all this. Modern science has largely removed the wonder of creation, giving us instead an exhausting stack of academic textbooks and scientific studies. But when Job was struggling with the personal tragedies and infirmities that God had allowed and the perceived injustice of it all, God never addressed Job's whys. Rather, he reinstilled in Job a fear of him by pointing to the wonder of his creation through some of the most beautiful poetry ever written.[197]

"Where were you when I laid the earth's foundation?
　　Tell me, if you understand.
Who marked off its dimensions? Surely you know!
　　Who stretched a measuring line across it?
On what were its footings set,
　　or who laid its cornerstone—
while the morning stars sang together
　　and all the angels shouted for joy?
Who shut up the sea behind doors
　　when it burst forth from the womb,
when I made the clouds its garment
　　and wrapped it in thick darkness,
when I fixed limits for it
　　and set its doors and bars in place,
when I said, 'This far you may come and no farther;
　　here is where your proud waves halt'? ...
Can you bind the chains of the Pleiades?
　　Can you loosen Orion's belt?
Can you bring forth the constellations in their seasons
　　or lead out the Bear with its cubs?
Do you know the laws of the heavens?
　　Can you set up God's dominion over the earth? ...
Do you know when the mountain goats give birth?
　　Do you watch when the doe bears her fawn?
Do you count the months till they bear?

Do you know the time they give birth?
They crouch down and bring forth their young;
    their labor pains are ended."[198]

Fast forward to the first century when Jesus's disciples had an encounter with creation they never forgot. After teaching all day, Jesus instructed them to get into a boat and cross the Sea of Galilee to the other side to escape the crowds. He was exhausted and immediately fell asleep in the stern of the boat. They hadn't gone far when a furious squall arose, and waves were crashing over the gunnels, threatening to sink the boat. These seasoned sailors knew the fury of the sea and saw their perilous situation. Perhaps they decided they could use another pair of hands for they awoke Jesus. The storm that scared the wits out of these veteran seamen had rocked Jesus to sleep. How deliciously ironic!

Jesus's response was most unexpected. He stood up and rebuked the wind and the waves, telling them to be still. I like to think that the sea, who may not have heard the Savior's voice since the dawn of creation, glanced up and said, "Sorry, boss, didn't know it was you!"

Immediately, the wind and sea calmed. Then the real fear struck these disciples. "They were terrified [literally, feared with great fear] and asked each other, 'Who is this? Even the wind and the waves obey him!'"[199] The terror of nature's fury was replaced with the fear of the One who had stilled it. It was one thing to be afraid of imminent drowning; it was quite another to see the power of the Creator. The disciples were terrified that they were in the presence of someone whom even the wind and waves obeyed.

We have a natural fear of the truly supernatural, and this was no different. The disciples displayed an instinctive fear of a power they did not yet understand. It was fear, but not the proper fear of Abba. It was only later, after they had witnessed the incredible love of Jesus on the cross, after his resurrection, after they had been filled with the Holy Spirit, after they began to reflect on their amazing three years with Jesus and began writing about it that they would develop a proper fear of Abba, a true fear of God—but one that was infused with God's love, was filled with wonder and awe, and that trusted his character.

Nevertheless, several times the disciples experienced this stark terror, and we cannot but conclude that these events were part of God's master plan. When Jesus came walking to them on the water in the dead of night as they were straining at the oars and getting nowhere, they were also filled with fear, thinking he was a ghost.[200] Shortly before Jesus's death and resurrection, he took Peter, James, and John up on a high mountain where he was transfigured before them and "his face shone like the sun, and his clothes became as white as the light." Moses and Elijah also appeared, talking with Jesus. Then a voice from "the cloud said, 'This is my Son, whom I love; with him I am well pleased. Listen to him!'" Upon hearing this, the disciples "fell facedown to the ground, terrified."[201]

In both situations, Jesus told them, "Don't be afraid." He did not want them to view him with such terror; he did not want them to react with instinctive fear but with a proper fear of Abba. Yes, seeing Jesus in his heavenly glory with his face shining like the sun was terrifying, but his love for his disciples was unquestioned and therefore the disciples should trust him implicitly.

The disciples' faith-journey was still in its infancy, and these events, orchestrated by a loving and compassionate Father, were the starting line in their quest to "understand the fear of the LORD and find the knowledge of God,"[202] a process we discussed in chapter one. It was only later that the apostle John wrote, perhaps reflecting on the incident on the Mount of Transfiguration, "we have seen his glory, the glory of the One and only Son, who came from the Father, full of grace and truth."[203] This event no longer brought him stark terror; it too had been transfigured into the fear of Abba, a fear full of grace and truth.

The power of our Creator revealed in his creation, in our lives, and in the lives of others can be the genesis in this holy quest of molding a healthy fear of Abba, a fear enveloped with his love. King David saw this marvelous union between the inspiration of God's creation, the unfathomability of God's love, and the inevitable fear and awe of God's power when he wrote, "For as high as the heavens are above the earth, so great is his love for those who fear him."[204]

One of my hobbies is woodworking, and one of the more dangerous tools in any woodshop is the table saw, which injures thousands of woodworkers every year, including a friend of mine who lost part of his finger. Seeing the danger, I decided to replace my saw with a SawStop table saw. Its newly patented safety technology instantly stops the saw's blade from turning if it touches my finger or any part of my body. I bought the saw from a nine-fingered salesman! There is a unique and undeniable credibility that is possessed by nine-fingered salesmen. They can warn us of danger, and they have the scars to back it up.

The Bible is full of nine-fingered salesmen and their powerful faith-stories. The Holy Spirit can use these personal stories to teach others the fear of Abba. For instance, Jesus and his disciples crossed the Sea of Galilee in a boat and landed in an area where the Gerasenes lived. Their city, Gerasa, was part of a larger conglomerate of cities known as the Decapolis.[205] Upon landing there, Jesus was immediately confronted with a man possessed by evil spirits. This man had been living in the tombs. He possessed extraordinary strength; he had broken chains and shackles that the people in the area had placed on him in their attempt to subdue his violent outbursts. Jesus cast the demons out of him and sent them into a nearby herd of pigs. The two thousand startled pigs then stampeded down the steep bank into the lake and drowned. Word spread fast about what had happened, and the village people quickly rushed to the scene. It wasn't the considerable loss of two thousand pigs that concerned them. Rather, "they saw the man who had been possessed by the legion of demons, sitting there, dressed and in his right mind; and they were afraid. ... Then the people began to plead with Jesus to leave their region." The undisputed evidence of the power of God was sitting in front of them, dressed and sane. But they were more afraid of the power that freed this man than the once crazy man himself, and the frightened people begged the Lord and Creator of the universe to leave their village.

The man pleaded with Jesus for permission to join him as he returned in the boat. Jesus did not let him, but said, "'Go home to your own people and tell them how much the Lord has done for you, and how he has had mercy on you.' So the man went away and began to tell in the Decapolis how much Jesus had done for him. And all the people were amazed."[206]

The people took a vote and evicted God from their village! Jesus knew they would not at this time listen to him, but he also knew that the passionate and personal gospel (good news) told by this newly transformed man was irrefutable. His chains had been broken, his spirit released, his life renewed, his joy restored, and his body clothed. He was a fully equipped, walking, breathing emissary with an undeniable story. This once crazy man was sent back to his own people who knew him or at least knew of him. So this "nine-fingered salesman," with no formal theological or missional training, who had not memorized any Scripture or attended any synagogue, who had not faithfully tithed or joined the choir or sung on the worship team, was sent out as Christ's first missionary to this region with a very simple message—just tell his faith-story; tell them what Jesus had done for him; tell them about his mercy. The man who had been infamous now famously communicated the indisputable good news of his healing and restoration. Apparently, the man did his job and did it well, for the next time that Jesus was in the region of the Decapolis, the people did not send him away. This time "some people brought to him a man who was deaf and could hardly talk, and they begged Jesus to place his hand on him," and Jesus healed him. [207]

The power of one's testimony can instill the fear of the Lord in others. King David, another "nine-fingered salesman," wrote:

I waited patiently for the LORD;
    he turned to me and heard my cry.
He lifted me out of the slimy pit,
    out of the mud and mire;
he set my feet on a rock
    and gave me a firm place to stand.
He put a new song in my mouth,
    a hymn of praise to our God.
Many will see and fear the LORD
    and put their trust in him.[208]

David had been trapped in the slimy pit of destruction, mud, and mire, perhaps after his adulterous sin with Bathsheba, but he cried out to God, and God reached down, lifted him out, and put him on solid ground. Then this "nine-fingered salesman" decided to go public with his story and even wrote a song about it for all of Israel to sing.

There were immediate responses to David's testimony: many saw what God had done, feared the Lord, and then trusted in him. Trusting God is the inevitable result of the proper fear and love of Abba. And then he put a new, unsung song in his mouth, a new hymn of praise to his God.

The fear of Abba changes us, changes others, changes our relationship with God, and even changes the purpose of our worship, as we will see in the next chapter.

 POINTS TO PERSONALIZE

- As we repeatedly ponder in our hearts the love of God for us, and as we recall the many times we have sinned and fallen short, we will realize that God's grace is unmerited and his mercy is overwhelming. Then we can echo the psalmist who wrote, "But with you there is forgiveness, that you may be feared."[209]

- The fear of God is an incredible gift from him, but as we grow in the fear of God, we must also deal with any idolatry in our lives that Scripture refers to as a divided heart: "Give me an undivided heart, that I may fear your name."[210]

- It is important that we choose to act and obey the instructions Jesus gives us, for if we don't, we are like the foolish man in Jesus's parable who builds his house without any foundation.

- Contemplating God's creation, under the guidance of the Holy Spirit, inspired King David to fear Abba. Our personal study of the human body, our earth, and the greater universe can do the same for us. As we come to better understand God's mighty power and his amazing grace, we will develop a healthy fear of Abba, a fear enveloped with his love.

 POINTS TO PONDER

- Are you ensnared by the love of money? If so, what does that look like in your life? What are some specific steps you can take to ensure God is your master and not money?

- Are there other idols in your life? Prestige? Lifestyle? Accomplishments? Addictions? What have they done for you? What can you now do to dethrone them so God has his proper place in your life?

- What about the power of God and creation inspires you to fear him?

9

INSPIRED TO WORSHIP

What a wretched man I am! Who will rescue me from this body that is subject to death?

Romans 7:24

But you are not controlled by your sinful nature. You are controlled by the Spirit if you have the Spirit of God living in you. (And remember that those who do not have the Spirit of Christ living in them do not belong to him at all.)

Romans 8:9 NLT

Not too long ago, my wife started up our Chevy Suburban, put it in drive, and it failed to move. Nothing was wrong with the engine or the tires; the transmission had gone out and needed to be replaced. It did not matter how pretty the vehicle looked, how well the engine was running, or how new the tires were. Without a working transmission, the vehicle was useless since the power of the engine could not be transferred to the tires.

The Holy Spirit is our spiritual transmission that takes the power of the Word of God and transmits it into our everyday life. Without a working transmission, filled with the oil of the Holy Spirit, our attempts to live a godly life or embrace the fear of Abba will be futile. The Word of God tells us how to live, how to treat each other kindly, and what is sinful and what is honorable, but only the Holy Spirit, our spiritual transmission, enables us to live a life worthy of the calling we have received.

Unfortunately, our spiritual transmission has an oil leak and needs to be regularly refilled. The apostle Paul says, "be filled with the Spirit, speaking to one another with psalms, hymns, and songs from the Spirit. Sing and make music from your heart to the Lord."[211] The Greek verb used in this passage for "be filled" implies a continual refilling; be filled again and again, and this is done through singing and making music in our hearts to the Lord.

David received a new revelation of the compassionate power of God who had raised him up from the slimy pit of destruction, out of the miry clay, and placed his feet on solid ground. This embrace of the tender fear of Abba was the inspiration for another hymn of praise that he wrote, Psalm 40. David said that God "put a new song in my mouth, a hymn of praise to our God."[212] We find in Scripture that the fear of the Lord imparts a new unveiling of God's character, and this becomes the inspiration for worship. This spiraling upward progression—from the fear of Abba to revelation to worship to a greater fear of the Lord—is extremely important if we are to "worship God acceptably with reverence and awe."[213] To see this in action, consider the prophet Jonah.

The Upward Spiral

The Case of Jonah

Jonah wasn't a seaman, but he saw the terror in the eyes of these salty sailors. He had never built a boat, but he could tell that this ship was close to breaking apart. He had encountered storms but had never experienced the increasing fury of one like this. Jonah knew that this was no ordinary storm; rather it was a physical manifestation of the literal wrath of God directed toward him because he had defied God's command to warn the people of Nineveh, the capital of the Assyrian nation and Israel's archenemy, of God's impending judgment. The sailors cast lots in search of the cause of the storm, and the lot fell on Jonah. This only revealed what the prophet already knew: he was the one to blame for the storm.

The divine rage that Jonah had hoped would be focused on Nineveh was now set on him. He was in the crosshairs of God's fury, not the Assyrian nation that had committed so many atrocities against the Hebrew people. Jonah knew that these sailors were innocent bystanders but that they would all soon perish because of his defiance. He felt that his death might assuage God's wrath, so he instructed the sailors to throw him overboard. He was unwilling to do the deed himself, perhaps thinking that the act of suicide was even more terrible than what he had already done.

The sailors, who had more personal integrity than Jonah, refused to throw him in the sea and tried to make land instead, all to no avail. The storm only grew worse. Finally, with no other option, they asked forgiveness of Jonah's God and cast him overboard where they had already thrown their precious cargo to lighten the ship. As the disobedient prophet sunk into the depths of the sea, the sailors saw the storm cease its raging. Then their fear of the storm was replaced by their fear of the God who had sent and calmed it. They now worshiped Jonah's God with vows and sacrificial offerings.[214]

Jonah was oblivious to all this as he slipped beneath the surface of the waves. Seaweed wrapped around his head as he sank down "to the roots of the [underwater] mountains," convinced that his life was over and that he would forever be banished from God's sight.[215]

Then, in one of the more peculiar scriptural twists, God sent a great fish to swallow Jonah, and he spent the next three days and nights without food or fresh water in this creature's belly. All this he recognized as the provision and mercy of God. He realized as he was getting weaker that his life was ebbing away, but he remembered the Lord, and his repentance, prayer, and worship rose to God's holy temple. He said, "But I, with shouts of grateful praise, will sacrifice to you. What I have vowed I will make good. I will say [to the Ninevites], 'Salvation comes from the LORD.' "[216] His newly found fear of the Lord revealed a new dimension of God, that the salvation that comes from the Lord is for all people (even Israel's enemies). Just as it did for King David, this revelation inspired new worship.

The sea creature vomited Jonah onto dry ground. Then this penitent prophet obeyed God, journeyed to Nineveh, and delivered God's message. The city, from the king down to the common peasants, repented and received God's salvation.

Numerous times in Scripture we see the fear of the Lord creating a new revelation of God and followed by new worship.

The Exodus

The children of Israel crossed the Red Sea, walking across on dry land with walls of water on their right and on their left and then witnessed the drowning of Pharaoh's army. "And when the Israelites saw the mighty hand of the LORD displayed against the Egyptians, the people feared the LORD and put their trust in him and in Moses his servant."[217] Then they sang a new song to the Lord, the song of Moses. Through the fear of Abba, they discovered a God they could trust because he loved them, and a new hymn was written and sung about this. Once again, the fear of God, the love of God, and the trust in God go hand in hand and all are commemorated in the song of Moses.

"Who is like You among the gods, LORD?
Who is like You, majestic in holiness,
Awesome in praises, working wonders?"[218]

A Babylonian King

Through the fear of the Lord, King Nebuchadnezzar discovered the Most High God whose "kingdom is an eternal kingdom" and "his dominion endures from generation to generation."[219] This king "praised the Most High" and "honored and glorified him."[220] His poem of praise was read to all the people throughout his vast empire.

Prophetic Visions

In a vision, the prophet Isaiah saw the Lord "high and exalted, seated on a throne; and the train of his robe filled the temple. ... The doorposts and thresholds shook and the temple was filled with smoke."[221] Isaiah cried, "Woe to me, for I am ruined! Because I am a man of unclean lips, and I live among a people of unclean lips; for my eyes have seen the King, the LORD of armies."[222] The fear of the Lord revealed to Isaiah the King over all, the Lord Almighty. Later, the Lord would also reveal to him more divine names, such as "Wonderful Counselor, Mighty God, Everlasting Father, [and] Prince of Peace."[223] Isaiah would write about all of this and more in his prophetic, lyrical praise that billions of people worldwide have now read.

Jesus's Disciples

Jesus's disciples were in a boat in the middle of the Sea of Galilee when a fierce storm arose. Jesus came to them, walking on the water. When he climbed into the boat to join them, the wind died down, the storm subsided. "Then those who were in the boat worshiped him, saying, 'Truly you are the Son of God.'"[224] Jesus most commonly referred to himself as the Son of Man, but the fear of the Lord revealed Jesus in a new way to his disciples. They now saw him as the Son of God, and they worshiped him.

The Judgment to Come

In the book of Revelation, the angels who "had the eternal gospel to proclaim to those who live on the earth—to every nation, tribe, language and people," cried out in a loud voice, "Fear God and give him glory, because the hour of his judgment has come. Worship him who made the heavens, the earth, the sea and the springs of water."[225] The fear of God reveals the God of impending judgment and creation, culminating in worship and giving him glory.

In Revelation, those who had been victorious over the beast were given harps, and they sang the song of Moses, a song that the apostle John recognized:

> "Great and marvelous are your deeds,
>   Lord God Almighty.
> Just and true are your ways,
>   King of the nations.
> Who will not fear you, Lord,
>   and bring glory to your name?
> For you alone are holy.
> All nations will come
>   and worship before you,
> for your righteous acts have been revealed."[226]

The fear of the Lord revealed to them the Lord God Almighty, the King of the nations, and they worshiped him and brought glory to his name.

Revelation and Fear

After four hundred years of slavery, God knew he would be making a "big ask" of the children of Israel. They would need to trust him, for they would have to leave the security of their homes and set off on foot into the desert. As we discovered in the Lord's Prayer, the love of our Abba, who is in heaven, whom we fear for his name is holy, is also someone we can trust and proclaim, "Thy kingdom come, thy will be done." The love of God and the fear of God naturally produce a trust in God, for who wouldn't trust someone whose love is unlimited and whose power is unfathomable? And so it would be with the Hebrew slaves.

"He [Moses] also performed the signs before the people, and they believed. And when they heard that the LORD was concerned about them and had seen their misery, they bowed down and worshiped."[227] God had given to Moses certain signs that he was to perform for the people: he was to throw his staff on the ground where it became a frightful snake and then, once picked up, became his staff again; he was to place his hand inside his cloak, and when withdrawn, it was covered with dreadful leprosy, and when returned back inside his cloak, his hand became normal.[228] These weren't the hugely popular miraculous signs that Jesus later performed—turning water into wine, healing the sick, or multiplying loaves of bread. No, the miraculous signs that God gave Moses were intended to instill the fear of God in the Hebrew people, and then once they also "heard that the LORD was concerned about them and had seen their misery," they bowed and worshiped this newly revealed Yahweh that they feared, loved, and trusted.

So it is with us. The worship of God that flows from us is formed by the names and character of God that have been revealed to us.

Living Water

> On the last and greatest day of the festival, Jesus stood and said in a loud voice, "Let anyone who is thirsty come to me and drink. Whoever believes in me, as Scripture has said, rivers of living water will flow from within them."[229]

Water is precious, but Jesus's gift of *living* water is priceless and only given to those who believe in him *as the Scripture has said*. What does Scripture say about Christ? He's "the Alpha and the Omega, the First and the Last, the Beginning and the End"[230]; he's "the pioneer and perfecter of faith"[231]; he's the "bread of life," the "Son of God," and the "Ancient of Days"[232]; the "son of man with a crown of gold"[233]; "Immanuel," our "Savior," our "Wonderful Counselor, Mighty God, Everlasting Father, Prince of Peace"[234]; he's our "Redeemer," "the Root and the Offspring of David, and the bright Morning Star," "the resurrection and the life," and the "King of kings and Lord of lords."[235]

Only someone who has received the covenantal fear of Abba truly recognizes the authority of Scripture, is obedient to it, and can therefore believe in Jesus "as the Scripture has said." But for those people who have no fear of Abba, the whole worship experience can be unsettling and strange. They don't understand what all the fuss is about since the Spirit of God has not yet indwelled them and Christ's living water has not refreshed them.

So what exactly is the living water? The apostle John goes on to explain what Jesus meant: "By this he meant the Spirit, whom those who believed in him were later to receive. Up to that time the Spirit had not been given, since Jesus had not yet been glorified."[236] But this Spirit doesn't just enter into us; he also flows out of our heart in rivers of living water, and this is done in the form of worship. In Ephesians, we are instructed to "be filled with the Spirit, speaking to one another with psalms, hymns, and songs from the Spirit. Sing and make music *from your heart to the Lord*, always giving thanks to God the Father for everything, in the name of our Lord Jesus Christ."[237]

Water is often used as a symbol of worship. The Levitical priests were instructed to pour out drink offerings every day before the Lord.[238] While a fugitive from King Saul, David yearned for a drink from the well of his hometown, Bethlehem, where Saul's army was encamped. David's three mighty men overheard that sigh and snuck through Saul's sentries, drew some water from the well, and brought it back to David who poured it out as a drink offering to the Lord.[239]

Earlier in Jesus's ministry, he used the phrase "living water" when speaking to the Samaritan woman at Jacob's well. Jesus said to her, "If you knew the gift of God and who it is that asks you for a drink, you would have asked him and he would have given you living water." Later in the conversation with her, he said that those who are true worshipers (those who have received his living water) will worship the Father in the Spirit and in truth.[240] Jesus's living water not only fills and satisfies our thirst for life, but this water flows out of us to the benefit of us and others and this is evidenced through our worship.

Water has another very unusual property. While it is soft and gentle as well as nourishing and life-giving, it also molds and shapes us much like the river rock that has lost its sharp edges due to the water's work. Author, pastor, and worship leader Glenn Packiam says: "Worship is not merely the expression of our faith, it is an essential part of what forms our faith. The way we worship becomes the way we believe."[241] Music inspires us, but worship transforms us through the indwelling power of the Holy Spirit, God's holy transmission. Just as water reshapes the ground and rock it flows over and through, so the Spirit-infused living water that comes from Jesus reshapes us as it wells up within us, especially through our worship of him.

Now the worship of God must follow his worship protocol: "Therefore, since we are receiving a kingdom that cannot be shaken, let us be thankful, *and so worship God acceptably with reverence and awe*, for our 'God is a consuming fire.' "[242]

Several years ago, I flew into another city and a driver picked me up at the airport. As we got to know each other, I discovered that his father was the minister of protocol for an African country. The person in this position instructs those who visit the president as to their nation's customs and the proper diplomatic etiquette when entering his presence. Certain things are simply not to be said or done in front of the president of this country.

God, too, has a protocol when entering his presence. We are to "enter his gates with thanksgiving and his courts with praise."[243] For this worship to be acceptable to God, it must be done with *reverence and awe.* The worship of our mighty God cannot be cavalier; there must be a sense of propriety. It must follow his protocol, not ours, and this protocol must convey the respect and honor that is rightfully due the Creator of this vast universe, for our God is a consuming fire. As King David wrote, "But I, by your great love, can come into your house; in reverence I bow down toward your holy temple."[244]

When we worship the Lord, we often celebrate his amazing grace; we thank him for being a good Father, for loving us and caring for us; and we exhort ourselves to bless the Lord and worship his holy name for there must be at least ten thousand reasons to do so. However, not many worship songs describe a God who is a consuming fire, not many admonish us to "serve the LORD with fear, and rejoice with trembling,"[245] and not often do we physically bow down in reverence to God.

Imagine the following scene. Two newlyweds are sitting in their living room for their first Christmas gift exchange. A fire is burning in the fireplace, lights and decorations adorn their Christmas tree, and each present under the tree is beautifully wrapped. The excited husband can't wait for his wife to unwrap his presents to her, so she goes first. She tenderly unwraps the first present, opens the box, and pulls out a power drill. The next gift she unwraps is a new golf driver. The next gift is a set of wrenches. With each opened present, the husband gets more and more excited, and the wife's puzzlement grows ever deeper as it becomes obvious that her selfish husband only bought gifts for her that he wanted.

Unfortunately, that sometimes describes our worship to God. Our gift of worship is often based upon what we prefer rather than what God wants. The style of music is one that *we enjoy*. The lyrics sometimes extol an awesome God, but he is awesome so that he can do awesome things *for us*. If we are not careful, our worship can inadvertently become quite narcissistic—we enjoy the worship time in church if it moves us. Whether it pleases God is sometimes secondary or not even a consideration.

Our worship of God must focus on God, the object of our worship, and not on our desires, needs, and wants. We must know the reason and purpose of our worship; the whys of worship must be clear: "I praise you *because* I am fearfully and wonderfully made; your works are wonderful, I know that full well"; "*Because* your love is better than life, my lips will glorify you"; "*Because* you are my help, I sing in the shadow of your wings"; "I will give thanks to the LORD *because* of his righteousness; I will sing the praises of the name of the LORD Most High"; "Praise be to the Lord, the God of Israel, *because* he has come to his people and redeemed them."[246]

The Molding Power of Worship

The living water of our worship molds and shapes us. Therefore, considerable thought must go into the structure of the worship service, or over time, we will be malformed.

How would our worship change if it were always filled with thanksgiving, reverence, and awe, knowing that *our God is a consuming fire*? How would the living water of our worship change if forged by a full revelation of the names of Christ as described in Scripture?

The psalmist wrote, "Blessed are those who have learned to acclaim you."[247] Worship is a skill we learn, a craft that is full of the blessings of God. And awe-filled worship is learned more easily and comes more naturally to those with a proper fear of Abba. When the fear of the Lord comes through worshipers, their worship "Proclaim(s) the power of God, whose majesty is over Israel, whose power is in the heavens,"[248] and they encourage others to do as they have done, to "sing to God ... who rides across the highest heavens, the ancient heavens, who thunders with mighty voice."[249] They extol the Lord, saying, "No one is like you, LORD; you are great, and your name is mighty in power. Who should not fear you, King of the nations? This is your due."[250]

Our worship time should reverentially extol a God we fear who is full of love, mercy, and grace, for the fear and love of Abba only serve to amplify each other, and they in turn form a trust in him.

Many of the writers of the historical hymns and many of today's artists understand this wonderful, synergistic relationship between the fear, love, and trust in God. Here is an example of a beautiful song written by Mary Maclean, an excellent song writer, that extols the greatness of God and then uses those attributes to illustrate God's unique and baffling love for each of us.

You who made the mountains and the sea
Measured out the universe and You made me
Echoes of the voice that called the worlds to be
Reach throughout the ages and now speak to me
You're my Creator King

You who made the valleys and the skies
Displayed Your love on far horizons and before my eyes
You who lit the stars and set the dawn in time
Called them all by name and now You whisper mine
You're my Creator King

Chorus
Who am I that You are mindful of me?
Who am I that You set Your love on me?
You're my Creator King

You who made the darkness and the light
Sun and moon to watch the day and guard the night
The hand that stretched the Heavens like a canopy
Reaches down to cover and watch over me
You're my Creator King[251]

Part of God's worship protocol is found in the proper preparations to worship. God does not want us to blissfully waltz into his sacred place as if we are entering a concert hall or a movie theater. Wherever the holy place is, whether at home, in the car, on a walk, or in a church sanctuary, our worship time with God should be preceded with a confession of our sin and a heartfelt commitment to trust in God alone.

Who may ascend the mountain of the LORD?
Who may stand in his holy place?
The one who has clean hands and a pure heart,
who does not trust in an idol
or swear by a false god.[252]

We can "then approach God's throne of grace with confidence, so that we may receive mercy and find grace to help us in our time of need,"[253] and we can say like King David, "But I, by your great love, can come into your house; in reverence I bow down toward your holy temple."[254] Our worship will then join with the heavens in a harmonious symphony of praise of a God of wonders whose love is "higher than the heavens" and whose "faithfulness reaches to the skies,"[255] a God who is holy and awesome and greatly feared.

The heavens praise your wonders, LORD,
your faithfulness too, in the assembly of the holy ones.
For who in the skies above can compare with the LORD?
Who is like the LORD among the heavenly beings?
In the council of the holy ones God is greatly feared;
he is more awesome than all who surround him.
Who is like you, LORD God Almighty?
You, LORD, are mighty, and your faithfulness surrounds you.[256]

God's Word is applied to our hearts through the transforming power of the Holy Spirit—God's holy transmission—and we are filled and refilled with this Spirit through reverential, awe-filled worship of our God whose love is boundless, whose power is infinite, and whose acts are trustworthy.

POINTS TO PERSONALIZE

- God's Word is powerful and transforms us with the help of the Holy Spirit so that we can become more loving, kind, patient, and gentle. The Holy Spirit is similar to the transmission of a vehicle since it takes the power of the Word of God and transmits it into our everyday lives.

- Our spiritual transmission is leaky and must be continually refilled, and this is done through worship. The apostle Paul wrote, "be filled with the Spirit, speaking to one another with psalms, hymns, and songs from the Spirit. Sing and make music from your heart to the Lord."[257]

- As we grow in our proper fear of God, we will also see him differently. In Scripture, God has many names that unveil the many aspects of his character, and this unveiling is important if we are to *"worship God acceptably with reverence and awe."*[258]

 POINTS TO PONDER

- What names of the Father, Son, and Holy Spirit have been revealed to you and how has that changed your worship? Here are a few: Savior, Lord, Prince of Peace, Mighty God, the Good Shepherd, Redeemer, Refuge, Hiding Place, the Everlasting Father, King of kings, Comforter, Counselor, and Lifter of My Head. Feel free to add to these others that you know.

- What about God will you now typically focus on in worship?

- Would you change your *preparation* for worship with what you now know? If so, what will you now do?

10

LEAVING THE BLANK, BLANK

"For the despairing man there should be kindness from his friend; so that he does not abandon the fear of the Almighty."
Job 6:14 NASB

The stories in the Gospel accounts of Jesus healing people contain interesting twists. Sometimes the sick person or his friend intently seeks out Jesus, and Jesus commends them for their faith. When blind Bartimaeus heard that Jesus was passing his way, he began to shout, "Jesus, Son of David, have mercy on me!" Jesus stopped, healed him, and told him "your faith has healed you."259 Other times it appears that the person receiving the healing possessed no faith at all. Jesus healed the man with the withered hand in the synagogue seemingly to prove a point to the religious leaders in attendance—that it's okay to do good and heal on the Sabbath.260 Jesus stopped a funeral procession of a widow who was about to bury her only son and, to the complete surprise of the mother, raised her son from the dead.261 Neither the man in the synagogue nor the mother requested prayer, and they most certainly had no healing expectations. Nevertheless, faith was always present at these healings even if only Jesus possessed it.

Faith is a fruit of the Holy Spirit. It is indisputable evidence that God is at work in our lives. "Now these three remain: faith, hope, and love. But the greatest of these is love."[262] Similar to the natural maturation of a fruit tree, the fruit of the Holy Spirit naturally develops as we mature in our faith.

But what exactly is faith? It is a trust in the person and power of God. Faith is an unwavering belief that God is great and God is good. It is not some magic, miracle formula. Rather, it is a deep-rooted confidence in the character of God and a willingness to obey him. And we know that those who fear God will always obey him. Therefore, faith is a natural result of the fear and love of God. If you want more faith, further develop the fear of the Lord within you by meditating on the awesome power of God and his infinite love for us.

I happened to attend a chapel service at a Christian university and heard the guest speaker tell the student body that illness was a direct consequence of their lack of faith and the sin in their lives. "Repent and you will be healed," he claimed. Fortunately, one of the theology professors had the boldness to stand up in the service and publicly question the speaker's distorted teaching. Nevertheless, much damage was done that day, and the school's chaplain office worked frantically to try to rein in the spiritual carnage that came from those statements. The chaplain later told me that one student had a vascular illness in his left arm. Despite his fervent and penitent prayers, he was not healed; he lost his arm, and he lost his faith.

If you have walked away from God or you know someone who has, it likely followed a time of personal crisis. Others have found that they emerged from a tragedy with a faith that has been strengthened and is profoundly more mature.

"I wouldn't trade the God I know now with the God I knew before; he is far more real now," reflected pastor Dave after he and his wife JoAnn recounted to me the heartbreaking story of the accidental death of their son Cory, a frolicking, fun-loving, nine-year-old kid. On March 14, 2011, while retrieving a gun from the family's gun safe, he mishandled the .22 rifle that he had safely used so many times before. His mother, JoAnn, heard the pop and ran downstairs to find Cory unconscious and bleeding from a serious head wound. Dave and JoAnn rushed him to the local medical center two miles away where he was quickly flown via Flight For Life helicopter to the nearest hospital. Despite their efforts, Cory died in route.

Now, nine years later, Cory's parents shared with me wisdom born from grief, so great that at times their only goal was to simply breathe and that was enough. "Tears are your friend, a good shower for your soul," mused JoAnn, and she would know. It was three months following Cory's death before she had a cry-free day.

Dave and JoAnn did not run from their pain or attempt to mask it. Instead, they embraced it. Dave explained: "This grieving time was my goodbye, and I did not want to miss any of it. I wanted to hurt like I should hurt. I wanted to live in the pain because I was saying goodbye to someone really important."

"Lots of people want to distract you from your grief, and they don't know that's not possible," JoAnn added.

"Time doesn't heal anything; it just gives you distance; only Jesus heals," Dave concluded. "We were so lucky to have Cory. God was so good to give him to us for nine years."

What caused these parents to emerge from this tragedy without a hint of bitterness and with a far greater love for God? "You have to trust that God can write your story better than you," pastor Dave explained. Such trust is born from an unwavering confidence in the awesomeness and fear of a God whose most tender affection for us is just as inexplicable as his unfathomable universe.

"Why would I be angry with God, the one person that I know can get me through this?" JoAnn wisely said as the previous nine years replayed in her mind.

As I reflected on Cory's death, I ended up expressing my thoughts in this poem:

Cory
7/23/2001–3/14/2011

What is said when breath of life
is taken from one so young,
When tomorrow's dreams are stilled
before they have begun?

What is said to God who chose to heal
a stretched-forth, withered hand
of one who had not prayed and
did not understand, yet
Did not heed the pleadings of a Dad
whose son succumbed to Adam's curse
and won't become a man?

God is great, and God is good
even when we can't explain
gifts to some, but not to all,
or choices He has made.

Our hearts must sing in praise of Him
who never wishes ill,
And kneel to Him who sometimes heals
But always loves us still![263]

When Jesus Christ came into our world, he also entered into our pain. He experienced the pain of Lazarus's death and wept. He probably experienced the pain of the death of his own earthly father, Joseph, since only his mother Mary is mentioned as present at his crucifixion when he charges his disciple, John, with caring for her.[264]

Jesus was authentically human. God's incarnation into humanity, through the person of Jesus Christ, was so complete and effective that those who knew him best, those from his hometown who had seen him grow up and mature, would not accept him as God. Their God was a mystical, powerful deity, not the kid down the street who apprenticed as a carpenter.

God's incarnation continues through us. When we invite God into our lives, he doesn't slap a coat of paint over us and call it good. Rather, he rebuilds us, starting with a new foundation and transforms us into a new creation. Our human DNA has not changed but our spiritual DNA displays the irrefutable evidence of a new heavenly Father. The change is profound, and from God's perspective, he has created us a second time: "Therefore, if anyone is in Christ, the new creation has come: The old has gone, the new is here!"[265] But those who know us best—our family and friends—may be just as dubious as those who lived in Jesus's hometown.

At the point that Job had lost everything—his wealth, his health, and his family—his three questionable friends arrived to set him straight. Job protested his innocence while they asserted that a just God would never inflict such suffering on a man without just cause. Perhaps the greatest sin of Job's friends was their lack of empathy for Job. Instead of sharing his suffering, they tried to explain why God had brought this grief upon Job. Rather than joining him in his pain, they attempted to justify it. Someone who is in crisis or deep despair does not need a theological exposition but simple acts of kindness. As Job exclaimed, "For the despairing man there should be kindness from his friend; so that he does not abandon the fear of the Almighty."[266]

People in crisis need a kind friend. They are at a spiritual crossroad in their life with two paths before them. The wide and obvious path, full of anger, fear, and resentment, leads them away from God, eventually to abandoning their faith or, as Job describes it, "forsaking the fear of the Almighty." The narrow and hidden path is not readily apparent, for not many tread here. It is sometimes only discovered with the kind help of a friend. It is a path of compassion, understanding, listening, love, forgiveness, and restoration. It is a path that is seldom walked alone.

Forgiving God

What test grade would you give to God for the way he is running this universe?

If you could rewrite his job description, would you?

Do you think he is fair and just?

Do you think he is a loving God, or is he largely to blame for this mess we call Earth where there is drought, famine, war, illness, broken homes, divorce, disease, earthquakes, and tsunamis?

If he is indeed all-powerful, couldn't he put an immediate end to all of this and, if so, why hasn't he?

The year was 2011, and a massive tsunami had just hit Japan. The lives of thousands had been tragically lost. Following the Sunday evening service, several of the church elders, including me, were standing in the front of the sanctuary and were available for prayer with anyone who wished. A woman came up to me and asked for prayer. She explained that she was having a difficult time "forgiving God" for this natural disaster. She questioned how a loving God who is big enough to create this universe and who has the power to control the weather, the wind, and the rain could kill so many innocent people.

Forgiving God—it's a strange concept, I thought. It implies that God has sinned and we, his creation, can grant or withhold from him needed forgiveness. I was struck by the unintended audacity in such a common statement. Rather than seeking forgiveness from God, *he* must now seek forgiveness from *us*? In this scenario, the roles have switched and the created are now judging their Creator.

I told the woman that when God created us, he instilled in us a sense of justice, a sense of right and wrong. "How is it," I asked, "that now we are using that very attribute to determine whether God himself is just?"

Did you catch the irony? With our own human limitations, we question the infinite goodness of the Creator who instilled in us our very sense of right and wrong. We pose the question, "How can a loving God _____?" Is this an appropriate question to ask of our Creator? I don't think so. In fact, I beg you, leave the blank, blank.

The apostle John tells us that "God is love."[267] Love is not something that God merely expresses. Love is the very essence of who he is. It is not an emotion he sometimes displays. He doesn't have good days and bad days. He doesn't wake up on the wrong side of the bed. Rather, he always acts in a loving way because he cannot act any differently. Love is his instinctual behavior because it is what he is.[268]

Some people might say, "How can a God who is all-loving and all-powerful send an earthquake and tsunami that killed hundreds of thousands of innocent men, women, and children? I just can't believe in a God like that." Their conclusion makes it sound as if their belief in God somehow makes him real.

Did God send it or was the tsunami just a natural consequence of an original creation that is broken because of sin? I want to think the latter because it is easier to square with my concept of a loving God. But then I am reminded that God did send Noah's flood (Genesis 6), Jonah's storm (Jonah 1:4), and Israel's famine (1 Kings 17:1). Honestly, I don't have an answer to the question.

By faith we must accept that God is love, and there are questions that will remain unanswered on this side of eternity. We must embrace the truth that God is great and God is good. As I have said before, understanding all the whys of God's activity is as futile as explaining calculus to my cat.

Job was in such pain that all he could do was sit in a heap of ash and scrape his boils with a shard of broken pottery. His wife was no help at all. She screamed at him, "Are you still maintaining your integrity? Curse God and die!" Job replied, "'You are talking like a foolish woman. Shall we accept good from God, and not trouble?' In all this, Job did not sin in what he said."[269]

We, too, must not sin in what we say. We tend to feel that God is good only if we can explain how he is good, as if God's goodness is limited by our understanding. It's a difficult thing to do, but if we are to continue to fear the Lord, we must leave the blank, blank.

Fearing God means acknowledging that he is God, "His greatness is unsearchable," and as far as the heavens are above the earth so are his ways higher than ours.[270] Since we cannot understand the mind of God, we must be okay with not explaining the inexplicable. When awed by God, "I don't know" is a perfectly good answer and is often the only appropriate one.

I don't know why thousands died in the 2011 tsunami that struck Japan, why some people are healed when prayed for and some are not, or why some children, like my mentally handicapped sister, are born with severe birth defects. I only know that if we fear God, some questions ought not to be asked if implied in the question is a dangerous irreverence.

For the Christian, fearing Abba should not be optional. We have studied the tremendous benefits and blessings associated with the fear of the Lord. We know that his steadfast love is toward those who fear him. We know that God confides in those who fear him and that he blesses these families for generations to come. But in Proverbs, God also warns the individual who repeatedly rejects his wisdom and correction, "since you disregard all my advice and do not accept my rebuke, I in turn will laugh when disaster strikes you; I will mock when calamity overtakes you … when distress and trouble overwhelm you. Then they will call to me but I will not answer; they will look for me but will not find me, since they hated knowledge and did not choose to fear the LORD."[271] Pretty sobering. Proverbs goes on to warn us that "When a man's folly brings his way to ruin, his heart rages against the LORD."[272] God is loving and patient, but at a point of his own designation and for his own just reasons, he turns away from those who refuse to heed his truth and wisdom and insist on living their own way. Such individuals may find fault with God when this happens, but the blame is not his to bear.

To the nation of Israel, which was about to be conquered and go into exile in Babylon for seventy years after many generations of evil and idolatry, God proclaimed through the prophet Jeremiah:

"Announce this to the descendants of Jacob
    and proclaim it in Judah:
Hear this, you foolish and senseless people,
    who have eyes but do not see,
    who have ears but do not hear:

Should you not fear me?" declares the LORD.

"Should you not tremble in my presence?

I made the sand a boundary for the sea,

an everlasting barrier it cannot cross.

The waves may roll, but they cannot prevail;

they may roar, but they cannot cross it.

But these people have stubborn and rebellious hearts;

they have turned aside and gone away.

They do not say to themselves,

'Let us fear the LORD our God,

who gives autumn and spring rains in season,

who assures us of the regular weeks of harvest.'" [273]

We tend to view the fear of Abba as an emotion, and emotions are unpredictable and influenced by outside forces that we often cannot control. But God views the fear of him as a choice we make, a conscious decision that is blatantly obvious if only we honestly examine his creation and not take for granted even the most rudimentary aspects of life, such as seasons, oceans, natural boundaries, and landmasses.

The people of Jeremiah's day did not have the knowledge of God's creation that we now possess. They did not know that the seasons of the year exist because God tilted the earth at exactly twenty-three and one-half degrees, thus changing the angle of the sunlight as the earth makes its way around the sun.

They did not know that the angle of our planet is kept constant because God also gave us just the right-sized moon that exerts the perfect amount of gravitational pull on the earth and that this moon also creates ocean tides that rise and fall twice a day, replenishing nutrients in coastal waters. [274]

They did not know that, unlike many other planets with elliptical orbits, our orbit around the sun is almost a perfect circle so that the amount of sunlight reaching us remains constant.[275]

They did not know that the galaxy we live in, the Milky Way, is a rare spiral galaxy with "arms" that spiral out from the center of the galaxy and that the earth is positioned in the only region of the "arm" that is hospitable to life.[276]

Ancient peoples would gaze up at the approximate nine thousand stars that a naked eye can see and not know that God created trillions of stars of different sizes, types, gases, and colors.

They may have felt the quiver of an earthquake but would not realize, as science has discovered, that "tectonic activity drives biodiversity; recycles chemicals, including carbon dioxide; and serves as a valuable force for maintaining a uniform temperature in the range for liquid water to exist."[277]

They did not understand the unusual properties of water whereby it floats when frozen rather than sink and that without this property ice would never melt and the earth would be a barren, frozen wasteland devoid of life.

Scientists have identified many such parameters that must simultaneously exist on the earth for life to also exist. In fact, Christian astrophysicist Hugh Ross has conservatively identified over four hundred parameters that must characterize a planet if it is to have the capability of supporting higher life-forms, such as the correct atmosphere, a sun that emits the correct form of sun light, planets that circle the earth that protect it from asteroids and comets, a thin earth's crust, the correct position in the galaxy, the right amount of gravity that keeps us on earth but does not crush us, and an electromagnetic field that allows life to function.[278]

If God expected the Jewish people of Jeremiah's day to fear him, with their elementary knowledge of his creation, we are certainly without excuse.

By the word of the LORD the heavens were made,
>their starry host by the breath of his mouth.
He gathers the waters of the sea into jars;
>he puts the deep into storehouses.
Let all the earth fear the LORD;
>let all the people of the world revere him.
For he spoke, and it came to be;
>he commanded, and it stood firm.[279]

 POINTS TO PERSONALIZE

- Faith is a trust in the person and power of God. A trust in God naturally develops when we contemplate his greatness and receive his love.
- Job exclaimed, "For the despairing man there should be kindness from his friend; so that he does not forsake the fear of the Almighty."[280] Simple acts of kindness are often the greatest gift we can give to someone who is experiencing a deep, personal crisis.
- "How can a loving God _____ ?" Fearing God means we must be willing to leave the blank, blank as difficult as that may be at times.

 POINTS TO PONDER

- How is faith a natural outcome of fearing and loving God?

- Have you or someone you know experienced a personal crisis and questioned the goodness of God? If so, how did it impact your relationship with God? What would you do differently now?

- Have you made the conscious decision to fear God? If so, what led you to make that choice? If not, what's holding you back?

11

HUMBLE PIE ... IT'S DELICIOUS

Humility is the fear of the LORD; its wages are riches and honor and life.

Proverbs 22:4

The fear and reverence of Abba are wonderful gifts we receive through the inspiration of the Holy Spirit as we encounter God's awesome power and are overwhelmed by the tenderness of his love and grace. These holy ingredients bond together to forge within us a proper fear of God. But how do we know if we have a healthy fear of God? Are there apparent traits or habits in our lives that help us self-diagnose our spiritual walk with him? Is there an evident quality in our life that one can identify?

The book of Proverbs says, "Humility is the fear of the LORD." In other words, true humility and the fear of the Lord are so similar that, much like identical twins, they are difficult to distinguish. The writer doesn't say that humility is a trait or a fruit or is evidence of the fear of God; he says that humility *is* the fear of God. If you find one, you will find the other, for they are inseparable.

But humility is unnatural. We typically desire, strive for, and declare our independence, not our dependence. We don't esteem humility. We esteem the self-made millionaires, those who have risen from nothing to great prominence, those who embody the American Dream of success and achievement. Our universities don't teach us to be humble either. There are no diplomas given out for humility.[281] It is not an ethos we honor. Few aspire to humility and yet that is what Jesus and all great servants of God possessed. For example, Moses is described as more humble than any other man. Mary, the mother of Jesus, speaking of herself said, "For He [God] has had regard for the humble state of His bond-servant [Mary]." The prophet Zechariah wrote when describing Jesus, "Behold, your king is coming to you; He is righteous and endowed with salvation, humble, and mounted on a donkey." In Jesus's only self-description, he said, "Take My yoke upon you and learn from Me, for I am gentle and humble in heart, and you will find rest for your souls."[282]

Humility Is a Choice

Humility is something we must actively seek and choose to embrace. Many times in Scripture we are admonished to humble ourselves. In a dream, the Lord spoke to King Solomon and said, "if my people, who are called by my name, will humble *themselves* and pray and seek my face and turn from their wicked ways, then I will hear from heaven, and I will forgive their sin and will heal their land." The apostle James writes, "Humble *yourselves* before the Lord, and he will lift you up." The apostle Paul, when describing Jesus, said, "And being found in appearance as a man, He *humbled Himself* and became obedient to the point of death, even the death of the cross."[283]

Humility is a conscious and deliberate act, a choice we make. Unlike salvation that is a gift from God that we receive, humility is an act and choice of man. God chose to send his only Son into the world and to have him bear the cost of our sin. God chose to redeem us and predestine us as his sons and daughters. But only we can choose the path of humility. It is a decision and choice God usually leaves to individual human beings.[284]

Humility is a choice to willingly take specific actions that create humility in one's heart. Jesus emptied *himself* and took on the form of a bondservant, a slave, a condition of humility.[285] To prepare for his ministry time in Corinth, Paul did not pull down the scrolls, read again the writings of the ancient prophets, and outline his three-point sermons. Rather, Paul when writing to the Corinthian church said, "I resolved to know nothing while I was with you except Jesus Christ and him crucified. I came to you in weakness with great fear and trembling."[286] Perhaps Paul had a fear of public speaking and that was the "thorn in the flesh" that he references in his second letter to the Corinthian church, the thorn that kept him humble and weak so he could be the chosen vessel of God's power. Whatever it was, with much wisdom Paul wrote, "I delight in weaknesses .... For when I am weak, then I am strong."[287] It is human nature to highlight our strengths, not our weaknesses. Paul chose the opposite. Not only was he self-aware of his weaknesses, but he exposed them and delighted in them for he knew that "God is opposed to the proud, but gives grace to the humble"[288] and that if he was to be a vessel of God's power and grace, continual humility, created by an ever-present and constant thorn-in-the-flesh reminder, was a prerequisite. For Paul, that "thorn" was a treasure because without it there would be no humility and therefore no grace, no fear of God, and no divine power in his life.

While we must choose humility, it's not a self-inspired choice. The Holy Spirit gives us the desire to be humble. We must never forget that the power of God—the same power that raised Christ from the dead—is constantly at work within us to mold and shape our lives.[289] Just as the transmission of a car transfers the power of the engine to the wheels, so the Holy Spirit infuses the power of the Word of God into our character, and this is often accomplished through life's trials, which teach us humility if we allow them.

What Humility Is and Isn't

Humility is not thinking less of ourselves but thinking of ourselves less. C. S. Lewis writes, "By this virtue, as by all others, [God] wants to turn the man's attention away from self to Him, and to the man's neighbors."[290] True humility is not low self-esteem and self-deprecation. Rather, it's a genuine recognition and celebration of the gifts and talents God has given to us and to our neighbors and a conscious and deliberate gratefulness for the awesome God who gifted us in these ways.

Much like the earth's magnetic field aligns a compass, the fear of the Lord aligns our character and creates in us true humility, for that is the only possible remaining human response to a God whose incredible majesty is displayed throughout all creation, who created us and breathed into us the breath of life, whose precious thoughts of us are as numerous as the sands of the sea, whose lovingkindness has forgiven our iniquity, whose mercy now extends beyond ourselves and to human generations yet unborn, whose faithfulness was established in heaven itself and is more predictable than the celestial orbits that drive our atomic clocks, and whose starry host was created by the breath of his mouth as he called them each by name.[291] Godly humility is not created by ruminating on our many failures but by seeing and meditating on God's greatness, thus creating in us the fear of Abba. This is why Isaiah cried out, "Woe to me, for I am ruined" when he saw a vision of the Lord seated on his throne, high and exalted, and why Peter, James, and John fell face down to the ground terrified when they heard the voice of God on the Mount of Transfiguration.[292] It is why the apostle John fell at Jesus's feet as though dead when he saw a revelation of him, and why Simon Peter fell down at Jesus's feet saying, "Go away from me, Lord, for I am a sinful man" after he witnessed the miraculous catch of fish.[293] All these physical acts of humility followed a manifestation of God's power.

Signs of Humility: The Case of Cornelius

Speaking of the children of Israel, God said to Moses, "Oh, that their hearts would be inclined to fear me and keep all my commands always."[294] The fear of Abba, humility, and obedience are always found together, work together, support each other, and enable each other. Job was described as "blameless and upright," a man who "feared God and shunned evil."[295]

Sometimes the humble person who fears God is the last person to come to that self-realization since humble individuals do not usually dwell on their humility. Such was the case with Cornelius, a Roman centurion who lived in Caesarea and whose story is recounted in the book of Acts, chapter ten.

Cornelius, a gentile, was "a devout man and one who feared God with all his household, and made many charitable contributions to the Jewish people and prayed to God continually." One of God's angels came to him in a vision and told him that his "prayers and charitable gifts have ascended as a memorial offering before God. Now dispatch some men to Joppa and send for a man named Simon, who is also called Peter; he is staying with a tanner named Simon, whose house is by the sea." Cornelius did as the angel commanded and sent three men to find the apostle Peter and bring him back to his house.[296]

While the three men were on the road, Peter had a vision that repeated to him three times that "What God has cleansed, no longer consider unholy." While he was pondering the vision, Cornelius's men arrived where Peter was staying. The Holy Spirit then said to Peter, "Behold, three men are looking for you. But get up, go downstairs and accompany them without misgivings, for I have sent them Myself." Peter obeyed, met the three men, and asked them why they wanted to see him. "They said, 'Cornelius, a centurion, a righteous and God-fearing man well spoken of by the entire nation of the Jews, was divinely directed by a holy angel to send for you to come to his house and hear a message from you.'" So Peter invited the travelers into the house and gave them lodging for the night.[297]

The next day Peter and some fellow believers left with the three men to go to see Cornelius. When they arrived at Cornelius's house, this Roman centurion was already anticipating their arrival. He had with him "his relatives and close friends. When Peter entered, Cornelius met him, and fell at his feet and worshiped him. But Peter helped him up, saying, 'Stand up; I, too, am just a man.' As he talked with him, he entered and found many people assembled. And he said to them, 'You yourselves know that it is forbidden for a Jewish man to associate with or visit a foreigner; and yet God has shown me that I am not call any person unholy or unclean. That is why I came without even raising any objection when I was sent for. So I ask, for what reason did you send for me?' " Cornelius then recounted his vision to Peter and told the apostle, "Now then, we are all here present before God to hear everything that you have been commanded by the Lord." Peter's response is telling, including how it speaks to the role that the fear of God played in this series of events:

Opening his mouth, Peter said: "I most certainly understand now that God is not one to show partiality, but in every nation *the one who fears Him and does what is right is acceptable to Him.* The word which He sent to the sons of Israel, preaching peace through

Jesus Christ (He is Lord of all)—you yourselves know the thing that happened throughout Judea, starting from Galilee, after the baptism which John proclaimed. You know of Jesus of Nazareth, how God anointed Him with the Holy Spirit and with power, and how He went about doing good and healing all who were oppressed by the devil, for God was with Him. We are witnesses of all the things that He did both in the country of the Jews and in Jerusalem. They also put Him to death by hanging Him on a cross. God raised Him up on the third day and granted that He be revealed, not to all the people, but to witnesses who had been chosen beforehand by God, that is, to us who ate and drank with Him after He arose from the dead. And He ordered us to preach to the people, and to testify solemnly that this is the One who has been appointed by God as Judge of the living and the dead. All the prophets testify of Him, that through His name everyone who believes in Him receives forgiveness of sins."

While Peter was still speaking these words, the Holy Spirit fell upon all those who were listening to the message. All the Jewish believers who came with Peter were amazed, because the gift of the Holy Spirit had also been poured out on the Gentiles. For they were hearing them speaking with tongues and exalting God. Then Peter responded, "Surely no one can refuse the water for these to be baptized, who have received the Holy Spirit just as we did, can he?" And he ordered them to be baptized in the name of Jesus Christ.[298]

First, it is helpful to know that the story of the Holy Spirit falling on the Roman centurion Cornelius and his household occurred perhaps six to eleven years after Jesus's death and resurrection and the initial filling of the Holy Spirit upon his disciples on the first day of Pentecost.[299]

From that time to the events at Cornelius's house, the new church was composed of Jews who had accepted Jesus as their Messiah and a much smaller number of gentile believers who had also converted to Judaism. The new church adhered to the Jewish dietary and ceremonial laws and customs. The assumption of the early Jewish Christians was that gentiles could not become Christians without first converting to Judaism and being circumcised. Prior to Peter's visit to Cornelius's house, Peter had never set foot in a gentile home, thinking of it and non-Jews as unclean. But God's plan of salvation included non-Jews too, and Cornelius was God's chosen person to receive this gentile Pentecost.

Why Cornelius? God could have chosen anyone. But when he scanned the souls of men and women to find the family for the first gentile outpouring of the Holy Spirit, he looked for someone who feared him. Cornelius did that. In fact, he not only feared God but so did his entire household, which would have included family members, servants, and even slaves. Furthermore, Cornelius's devotion to and fear of God were evident because of his prayer life and his love and concern for the poor. As the angel said to Cornelius, "Your prayers and alms have ascended as a memorial before God." David wrote many centuries before, "May my prayer be set before you [God] like incense."[300] Prayers and alms are likened to incense: they rise up, they permeate the air, and their fragrance cannot be ignored. When God searched for one who feared him, the unmistakable aroma of Cornelius's prayers and gifts to the poor kept drawing his gaze back to that home in Caesarea where the poor were loved and cared for and prayer was a daily habit. Perhaps the apostle Paul was thinking of Cornelius when he later wrote to the Philippian church, "in humility value others above yourselves, not looking to your own interests but each of you to the interests of the others."[301]

Job, who also feared God, said:

"Whoever heard me spoke well of me,

and those who saw me commended me,

because I rescued the poor who cried for help,

and the fatherless who had none to assist them.

The one who was dying blessed me;

I made the widow's heart sing."[302]

For over twenty-five years, my family has supported India Transformed, a marvelous Christian ministry to the poor of India. This ministry has provided Christian childcare to thousands of indigent children; empowered more than 2,500 impoverished women with new job skills; founded over 1,300 churches that have reached millions of Indians with the good news of Jesus Christ; and provided a Christian education to several thousand students through a school facility in Bangalore. If you are looking for an effective Christian ministry that is focused on the poor, the fatherless, and the widow, India Transformed is worthy of your serious consideration.[303] They exhibit through their work the fear of Abba. They live out what James describes: "Religion that God our Father accepts as pure and faultless is this: to look after orphans and widows in their distress and to keep oneself from being polluted by the world."[304]

Jesus warned of the dangers of false prophets—those who appear to be genuine but are really ferocious wolves dressed in sheep's clothing. He told his disciples that such individuals would be readily apparent once the bad fruit of their lives was identified. Jesus said, "every good tree bears good fruit, but a bad tree bears bad fruit."[305] Good fruit is the obvious and external evidence of an internal transformation. Likewise, where you find the fear of the Lord you will always find the fruit of humility, obedience, an intercessory heart, a love for others, and a tenderness and compassion for the poor, the fatherless, and the widow. The fear of God begins inside of us but never remains there. Like the fruit of love, it flows out of us and into what we say and do.

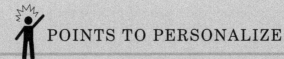

POINTS TO PERSONALIZE

- The fear of the Lord is evident by the fruit of humility in our lives. It is also evident by our compassion for the poor, the fatherless, the widow, our love for others, and our devotion to prayer.
- Many times in Scripture we are admonished to humble ourselves. Humility is a choice that we make, but the Holy Spirit gives us the desire to be humble. The Holy Spirit is at work within us to mold our character. As a car's transmission transfers the power of the engine to the wheels, so the Holy Spirit transfers the power of the Word of God to our daily lives.

POINTS TO PONDER

- Would your family and your closest friends describe you as a humble person? Consider asking them. Then be attentive to what they say, humbly receiving it. Record what you learn about their perception of you, and take it to God in prayer.

- What are some specific actions or steps you can take to cultivate humility in your life?

- Does your giving to the Lord reflect a tender heart toward the poor and others enduring hardships? If not, what are some steps you can take in the coming weeks to start to change this in your life?

12

PASSING IT ON

*Come, my children, listen to me; I will teach you the fear of the L*ORD.

Psalm 34:11

Many strange things have been handed down from one generation to the next through an inheritance, but perhaps none so strange as that found in the last will and testament of Napoleon Bonaparte, the nineteenth-century French emperor. In addition to the two hundred million francs, three palaces, furniture, books, bridles, saddles, pistols, swords, diamonds, snuff boxes, medals, china, linens, and clocks that he dispersed, he directed that the executor of his estate, Marchand, "shall preserve my hair, and cause a bracelet to be made of it, with a little gold clasp, to be sent to the Empress Maria Louisa, to my mother, and to each of my brothers, sisters, nephews, nieces, the Cardinal; and one of larger size for my son."[306] It was an unusual request.

The same could be said of the one item or trait that God wished that each generation would give to the next. God told Moses at Mount Sinai, "Oh, that their hearts would be inclined to fear me and keep all my commands always, so that it might go well with them and their children forever!"[307] God's inheritance list is short and simple—fear him and pass this on to the next generation so that our last will and testament contains an inheritance far more meaningful than bracelets braided from locks of our hair.

As we have found, a fear, awe, and reverence of God are very good for us to have. If we don't properly fear God, we won't obey him, and if we don't obey him, we will live a sinful life in rebellion against him. Virtually every problem in life—strained relationships, divorce, selfishness, greed, lust, anger, pride, war, poverty, to name but a few—can be traced back to sin. But sin in our lives can be traced one step further. We sin because we do not fear the Lord. Moses said to the Hebrews, "Do not be afraid. God has come to test you, so that the fear of God will be with you to keep you from sinning." Centuries later, King Solomon added, "Through love and faithfulness sin is atoned for; through the fear of the LORD evil is avoided."[308] God has always desired, especially for his people, that we fear him for our sakes, for that will motivate us to keep his commands and prepare us to receive his abundant blessings when and how he sees fit. The fear of the Lord is more important than an education, talents, discipline, title, wealth, or nobility, for only those who fear him "lack nothing."[309]

In our quest, we have discovered that the proper fear of the Lord is a foundational element of our faith and is necessary if we are to live a godly life and receive God's protection, compassion, provision, wisdom, mercy, God's riches, honor, and true life itself.[310] It is not possible to overstate the importance of the covenantal fear of Abba. Among other things, we have found that "the fear of the LORD leads to life; then one rests content, untouched by trouble." It engenders God's tender compassion, for just "as a father has compassion on his children, so the LORD has compassion on those who fear him."[311] It is life-giving and keeps us safe from satan's snares and from sin.[312] It is the beginning of wisdom and the foundation of a healthy marriage.[313] It inspires courage, obedience, and discipleship.[314] And it must also be the genesis of our worship.[315]

Given all that the fear of Abba does for us, why wouldn't we want to pass it along to future generations? It's among the greatest gifts we can give. How can we do this? Let's revisit some of the foundation we've laid before we dig into some ways to make the fear of the Lord an essential part of the inheritance we bequeath to others, especially to those we love and care for the most.

The Right Order

In chapter one, I laid out the principal found in Proverbs 2 that the quest to discover the fear of the Lord begins with accepting the authority of his Word and ends with understanding the fear of him. Jesus said it this way: "Anyone who chooses to do the will of God will find out whether my teaching comes from God or whether I speak on my own."[316] According to Jesus, the choice to obey comes first and revelation follows. Although it is contrary to human nature, *we must obey to understand, not because we understand*, and that sort of obedience to Christ requires faith—faith that the sovereign God with his incredible power created countless galaxies and stars that he calls by name, faith that this God of immense power is also a God of infinite love and that he knows you and me and loves us. This faith, instilled in us through the Holy Spirit, leads us to fear Abba, and the fear of Abba produces in us even greater faith. Recall that it wasn't until Jonah experienced the fear of the Lord firsthand that he had the faith to proclaim God's prophetic message in Nineveh. Jonah obeyed God, and God eventually explained to Jonah why he went to such lengths to save this evil city: "should I not have concern for the great city of Nineveh, in which there are more than a hundred and twenty thousand people who cannot tell their right hand from their left—and also many animals?"[317] Jonah obeyed to understand and that requires faith.

Human wisdom says that faith and fear cannot coexist; God's wisdom says that faith is forged through the fear of the Lord and embracing this fear is wise. King Solomon, the wisest man prior to Christ to walk this earth, wrote, "The fear of the LORD is the beginning of wisdom."[318]

So the right order in the fearing God process is:

- Accept Scripture as the inspired and authoritative Word of God.[319]
- Ask the Holy Spirit to use the Word of God to transform you.[320]
- Store up God's Word within you through meditation and memorization.[321]
- Study the greatness of God as revealed through Scripture and through the study of his amazing creation.[322]
- Choose the path of humility.[323]
- Infuse your worship of God with the proper fear of God.[324]
- Diligently exercise the holy habits of prayer, Scripture reading, regular tithing, carrying for widows and orphans, and gifts to the poor.[325]
- Live a courageous, faith-filled life knowing that you are a child of the Creator of this vast universe, the King of kings and Lord of lords, who is also your friend, whose thoughts of you outnumber the grains of sand, and whose love for you is higher than the heavens are above the earth.[326]

The Example of Jesus

Did Jesus exhibit the fear of Abba and wisdom? Yes, he did. Of course, he was (and is) the Son of God, so divine through and through. But he was (and still is) also human, and, according to Scripture, his wisdom as a man developed over time. Luke says, referring to Jesus's youth, that "Jesus grew in wisdom and stature, and in favor with God and man."[327]

From the time Jesus was twelve years old until he started his ministry at around age thirty, little is known about his life. We know that he lived in the small town of Nazareth and that his family was well known there.[328] We know that he learned to read and write and that the local synagogue was the center of learning. Perhaps, on a school day, this might have happened:

Jesus, a ten-year-old boy, is taking his daily walk to the synagogue in Nazareth. The dusty footpath leads him past his neighbors' small, two-room homes that are like his. In one room the family cooks and eats; in the other they all sleep. Jesus's home is unusual since his father also built a small carpentry and masonry shop where his father works long hours making tables, chairs, bowls, and carts. Wood is tough to come by in this arid part of northern Israel, and so his father also works as a stonemason constructing homes and other buildings. There is no shortage of stone.

Jesus's life is simple and happy. In the morning he spends four hours at the synagogue learning to read and write as he memorizes Scripture; in the afternoon he does his daily chores, helps his father where he is an apprentice learning his father's trade, s, friends, and cousin, John.

ript village in northern Israel. It is butes pass anywhere close to it. In kes a week of walking just to get to knows he will be making this trip to for the first time. His mother reminds temple once before, as a forty-day-old child.[329] While there, a prophet Simeon prophesized something[330] that mama says she will tell him when he is older.

He is thrilled as he thinks about the trip. It will be Passover time at the beautiful temple. The scribes and priests will quiz him and other boys on the Torah and the Prophets. If he passes, he will participate in his bar mitzvah and become a Jewish man.

Today, as he walks the dusty path, Jesus is excited since they are studying his favorite book, Isaiah. He has memorized large portions of Scripture and has excitedly discovered specific sections in the prophetic books that tell the story of his own birth. His mother and father have of course told him many times about the angels appearing to the shepherds on the hills of Bethlehem the night of his birth, the star that led the wise men to their home, the appearances of the angel Gabriel, and his family's flight to Egypt in the dead of night. He has often heard these stories, but it is still fun to read how Micah prophesized he would be born in Bethlehem and Isaiah predicted that he would be born in a special way (something about a virgin, whatever that is), live in the region of Galilee, where they now live, and be an heir to the throne of David![331]

The rabbi told his class yesterday that the passage they would study today is difficult to read and even more difficult to understand for no one really knows to whom the passage is referring. Jesus finds himself very intrigued to hear this Scripture for the very first time. Maybe he can solve the mystery that h baffled rabbis for years.

The boy enters the synagogue, finds his usual spot down. His rabbi begins reading from the prophet Isaiah

Who has believed our message
>and to whom has the arm of the LORD been revealed?

He grew up before him like a tender shoot,
>and like a root out of dry ground.

He had no beauty or majesty ... .

He was despised and rejected by mankind,
>a man of suffering, and familiar with pain. ...

Surely he took up our pain
>and bore our suffering,

yet we considered him punished by God,
>stricken by him, and afflicted.

But he was pierced for our transgressions,
>he was crushed for our iniquities;

the punishment that brought us peace was on him ... .

We all, like sheep, have gone astray,
>each of us has turned to our own way;

and the LORD has laid on him
>the iniquity of us all.

He was oppressed and afflicted,
>yet he did not open his mouth;

he was led like a lamb to the slaughter,
>and as a sheep before its shearers is silent,

so he did not open his mouth.

About halfway through the reading, Jesus suddenly realizes that this passage, written seven hundred years earlier, was not written about some obscure person or some persecuted prophet. No, the passage this rabbi is reading is his own obituary! This passage that has confused rabbis for hundreds of years is crystal clear to him. The words explode in his mind—a tender shoot, despised, rejected, stricken, afflicted, transgressions, crushed, and punished.

In tears he bursts out of the synagogue. Sobbing uncontrollably, he stumbles and retraces the well-worn path back to his home where he finds comfort in the loving arms of his mother. Mary weeps, too, as Jesus between sobs tries to explain what just happened, as best a ten-year-old can. She weeps as she watches her son becoming a man, a man of sorrows and acquainted with grief. She weeps as she recalls the prophetic words of Simeon to her, "and a sword will pierce your own soul too."[332] She knew this day would come ... just not today.

When God could have chosen any Jewish parents on earth, he chose Mary and Joseph to raise his Son. There was something very special about these parents. Joseph was an honorable man who obeyed God without hesitation. As we have discovered, an obedient heart is evidence of someone who fears and loves Abba. When the angel appeared to Joseph and told him to take his pregnant fiancé to be his wife, he obeyed, despite the unbelievable explanation that God had impregnated Mary, despite the public humiliation that would inevitably come from the wrong assumption that Mary had conceived Joseph's child out of wedlock, and despite the constraint that he could not consummate their marriage until after Jesus's birth. And when the angel appeared to Joseph a second time and told him to take his family to Egypt for a safe haven, he immediately packed up in the dead of night and left Bethlehem.

Mary had a profound understanding of the heart of her heavenly Father. In her poetic song of praise, we see a teenager filled with the knowledge of God who is wise beyond her years. She exclaims:

My soul glorifies the Lord

    and my spirit rejoices in God my Savior,

for he has been mindful

    of the humble state of his servant.

From now on all generations will call me blessed,

    for the Mighty One has done great things for me—

    holy is his name.

His mercy extends to those who fear him,

    from generation to generation.

He has performed mighty deeds with his arm;

    he has scattered those who are proud in their inmost thoughts.

He has brought down rulers from their thrones

    but has lifted up the humble.

He has filled the hungry with good things

    but has sent the rich away empty.

He has helped his servant Israel,

    remembering to be merciful

to Abraham and his descendants forever,

    just as he promised our ancestors.[333]

The Holy Spirit instilled in Jesus a delight in the fear of the Lord. And the fruit of the fear of Abba—wisdom, understanding, counsel, might, and knowledge—were evident in his ministry and in Mary and Joseph.

The Spirit of the Lord will rest on him—

    the Spirit of wisdom and of understanding,

    the Spirit of counsel and of might,

    the Spirit of the knowledge and fear of the Lord—

and he will delight in the fear of the Lord.[334]

Luke writes that Jesus "grew in wisdom and stature, and in favor with God and man."[335] Jesus's growth was well-rounded and complete. His body naturally developed and matured; his godly wisdom grew; and his relationships with the people who knew him and with his heavenly Father were marked with favor. God's favor rests on those who fear him, and Jesus took great delight in the fear of God. "His pleasure is not in the strength of the horse, nor his delight in the legs of the warrior; the LORD delights in those who fear him, who put their hope in his unfailing love."[336]

If our goal is to be conformed to the image of Christ, to be wise, to be pressed or molded into his likeness, and, like him, to exhibit the fruit of the Holy Spirit of love, joy, peace, patience, kindness, goodness, faithfulness, gentleness and self-control,[337] then, like Jesus, we must choose to fear Abba, and we must instill that in our children as well.

Catching and Teaching

The Psalmist wrote, "Come, my children, listen to me; I will teach you the fear of the LORD."[338] The fear of the Lord is both taught and caught.

It is *caught* when children witness their parents living their lives in obedience to God's Word. It is caught when the day-to-day activities in the home model the fruit of the Spirit. It is caught when the children see their parents serving each other, apologizing to one another for unkind actions, reading the Word of God together, and praying with and for each other. It is caught when children see a consistency between what is taught on Sunday morning and how life is lived Monday through Saturday. It is caught when the child witnesses the parent return the excess change that he or she inadvertently received at the grocery story. It is caught when parents exhibit healthy spiritual habits of regular prayer, quiet time, church attendance, and tithing, and when the inevitable unkind words are said, an apology is quick to follow. It is caught when children see their parents attending marriage and family seminars and reading books to better their parenting skills.[339] It is caught when children are disciplined in a consistently loving, compassionate, and unequivocal manner that reinforces the spiritual authority in the home that is given to parents, and especially the father.[340] It is caught when the children understand that their parents are not perfect but are godly nonetheless, and when the children become married adults, they realize that their goal is to emulate key aspects of their parents' marriage in their own.

The fear of Abba is also *taught*. Jesus taught through parables, or stories, and so can we. What are the faith stories of your life through which you learned to fear, love, and trust Abba? What are those key incidents in your life that forged your faith and gave you a profound reverence and awe of God? Have you taken steps to memorialize them so that you always remember?

Over thirty years ago, we created in our family what we call an Ebenezer box into which we have placed mementos of the Lord's love and faithfulness to us so that we would never forget them. When most of us hear the name "Ebenezer," we think of the character Ebenezer Scrooge in Charles Dickens's story *A Christmas Carol*. However, the name comes from the Bible and has a wonderful meaning to it. Following a victory over the Philistine army by the outnumbered and poorly armed Israeli army, the prophet Samuel knew he had to do something so that this miraculous story would be passed on from generation to generation. So "Samuel took a stone and set it up between Mizpah and Shen. He named it Ebenezer, saying 'Thus far the LORD has helped us.' "[341] Ebenezer, which means "stone of help," is a memorial that reminds us of what God has done for us. We need these physical reminders because our human nature tends to forget the things we should recall and remember the things we should forget.

Often in Scripture God instructs the children of Israel to remember him and what he did for them.[342] Even at the last supper, Jesus instructed his disciples to eat the bread and drink the wine "in remembrance of me."[343] The Psalmist writes, "I will remember the deeds of the LORD; yes, I will remember your miracles of long ago."[344] Like the prophet Samuel did for the Hebrews, we, too, need visible, concrete memory aids so that we can remember the deeds of the Lord and his miracles of long ago. This is why for many years now that our family has placed faith-mementos into our Ebenezer box. In there are sacred reminders that "the steadfast love of the LORD never ceases; his mercies never come to an end."[345]

When we open our Ebenezer box, among many other items, there is a small piece of wood with a nail through it to remind me of the time when I was eleven years old, fell out of my treehouse, and landed on my head just inches away from a board with an up-turned spike. In the box are the hospital bracelets for the births of our four children, and hospital bracelets for the three eye surgeries one child received. One of our kids drew a picture of a vehicle driving at night to remind us of the time when the driver of this car fell asleep at the wheel and ran off the highway into the ditch with three of our children in the back seat, and no one was injured. I have a small carbon rod in the box to remind me of the time in my youth when I was foolishly playing with electricity and was not injured or killed.

To be convinced of the protection, power, and love of our heavenly Abba, our family needs to look no further than our Ebenezer box, for it contains the physical evidence that proves our God is faithful even when we are not, that he can be trusted even when we doubt, and that he loves us with an infinite love that is "as high as the heavens are above the earth."[346]

There is no reason not to revere and fear a God who is unchangeably loving and trustworthy.

As you go through life, you should place into your box mementos of the Lord's miracles, protection, love, and faithfulness to you. Yes, there will be dark times in your life when you question his goodness. Remember that it is always the darkest before the dawn. And during those dark hours of the soul, go to your Ebenezer box, examine its sacred contents, and remind yourself of God's goodness. When you do, the awful darkness of the night will fade and dawn will come.

Most importantly, the fear of Abba is taught through the reading and application of the Word of God to our lives. The numerous passages and stories that I have cited in this book can serve as a fear-of-the-Lord foundation. Scripture is infused with the fear of Abba.

The kings of Israel were to take the reading of God's Word one step further. They were instructed to handwrite their own personal copy of the Torah, the law of God—all 304,805 letters,[347] a task that takes about one and one-half years.

> "When he takes the throne of his kingdom, he is to write for himself on a scroll a copy of this law, taken from that of the Levitical priests. It is to be with him, and he is to read it all the days of his life *so that he may learn to revere the* LORD *his God and follow carefully all the words of this law* and these decrees and not consider himself better than his fellow Israelites and turn from the law to the right or to the left."[348]

Learning to fear the Lord was so important that the first eighteen months of the new king's reign were to be devoted to reproducing his own private edition of God's Word.

Conclusion

Then those who feared the LORD talked with each other, and the
LORD listened and heard. A scroll of remembrance was written in
his presence concerning those who feared the LORD and honored
his name. "On the day when I act," says the LORD Almighty, "they
will be my treasured possession. I will spare them, just as a father
has compassion and spares his son who serves him."[349]

The Lord eavesdrops on the conversations of those who fear him
and honor his name. Then he takes notes, and a scroll of remembrance
is created in heaven, more for our benefit than his since he never forgets.
God is very protective of those who revere him. The psalmist says, "The
angel of the LORD encamps around those who fear him."[350] When that final
day is announced with a trumpet blast, and Jesus comes with compassion
to gather his treasured possession, his bride, from the four corners of the
earth to take us to the home he has been preparing for us for the last two
thousand years, he will have with him a scroll. On that scroll will be the
names of those who have chosen to fear Abba. These people will join the
saints that have already formed the heavenly choir that "fear God and give
him glory."[351]

> The LORD is exalted, for he dwells on high;
>> he will fill Zion with his justice and righteousness.
> He will be the sure foundation for your times,
>> a rich store of salvation and wisdom and knowledge;
>> the fear of the LORD is the key to this treasure.[352]

When we see God in all his glory, in the splendor of his holiness,
when we hear the 144,000 harpists playing a new song of praise to our

Mighty God and we witness the seraphim and archangels bowing and giving homage to the Lamb of God who sits on the throne, the wonder of his redeeming love for us will be overwhelming, and we, too, will bow in reverential fear and worship the Alpha and Omega, the King of kings and Lord of lords. The old earth will be done away with, and we will witness the creation of a new heaven and a new earth. And the eternal, awe-filled fear and worship of our heavenly Abba will have only begun. But even in eternity, we will never understand why our everlasting Father chose to set his love and affection on us, and we will wonder why we were ever afraid of fearing him.

 POINTS TO PERSONALIZE

- "Every good gift and every perfect gift is from above, coming down from the Father of lights."[353] Of all the gifts given to us by our loving heavenly Father, the fear of him is among the most precious and can only be understood within the context of our heavenly family. God, our Father, loves us, his children, so much that his greatest desire is for us to be enveloped by his love and astounded by his power and might so that we will implicitly trust and obey him in all things.
- "Come, O children, listen to me; I will teach you the fear of the LORD."[354] This gift is also something we can pass on to our children and is a wonderful family heritage.
- "The fear of the LORD is pure, enduring forever."[355] The pursuit of purity in our lives must begin with the fear of the Lord for it is pure. "Finally, brothers and sisters, whatever is true, whatever is noble, whatever is right, whatever is pure, whatever is lovely,

whatever is admirable—if anything is excellent or praiseworthy—think about such things."[356]

- The fear of the Lord endures forever. It is something we will take with us to heaven. "Then I saw another angel flying in midair, and he had the *eternal gospel* to proclaim to those who live on the earth—to every nation, tribe, language and people. He said in a loud voice, 'Fear God and give him glory.' "[357] In addition to salvation, the eternal gospel (good news) *must* also include the fear of God and the worship of him.

POINTS TO PONDER

- What physical mementos are you going to place in your Ebenezer box so that you remember the faithfulness of God and can teach this to your children or grandchildren?

- How has this book changed your walk and relationship with God?

ACKNOWLEDGMENTS

This book has been written because many people have poured into my life their wisdom and knowledge and have done so in gracious ways under the guidance of the Holy Spirit.

Most importantly, I want to thank my Lord and Savior, Jesus Christ, for providing a way, through his death and resurrection, to introduce me to his loving and mighty Abba. I have experienced firsthand what David wrote: "The LORD is compassionate and gracious, slow to anger, abounding in love."[358]

A very special thank you to Jenny, my wife of nearly forty years, my best friend and confidant. You have graciously encouraged me to live a life of obedience to God and to embrace the calling that he has placed on my life. "A woman who fears the LORD is to be praised,"[359] and you indeed deserve such praise. Thank you for your kind heart and never-ending love.

For the last thirty years, Rev. and Dr. Don and Judy Miles have been a constant source of encouragement and inspiration to my wife and me in all areas of our lives. Without them, it is doubtful that this book would have been written. He convinced me that, although I was a theological layman, I had a message for the church that was greatly needed, seldom taught, poorly understood, and was a missing foundation in the lives of most Christians. Don and Judy have been our mentors and friends, counselors and teachers. Thank you!

I also want to thank my parents, Oliver and Gene Carlson, and my father and mother in-law, Dick and Mary MacWherter, for living their lives in the fear of the Lord, praying for me, and providing to me an example of what it means to live in obedience to God.

Thanks to all of you who read through preliminary drafts of this book, including Dr. Michael Eckelcamp, Dr. Marty Meyer, Lowell Adrian, members of our Bible study group—Kirk and Julie, Lisa and Kelly, John and Stacey, and Mark—members of my men's Bible study group, and all the members of my Christian CEO forum.

Thank you, Bill Watkins, for editing a book of a first-time author and bringing clarity and direction to this book. Your professionalism helped craft this book so that it is meaningful and understandable.

Last, a special thanks to our adult children and their spouses, Liz and Josh, Jayne and Chris, Kyle and Kristina, and Ella for reading the manuscript and being an important sounding board as we discussed various aspects of the book around the dinner table or while sitting on the back porch in the evening in the light of our fireplace.

ABOUT THE AUTHOR

Nathan Carlson is the President of IndiaTransformed.org, a nonprofit organization dedicated to bringing the good news of Jesus Christ to the people of India and particularly to that nation's poor. This organization has provided funding for the training of over 1,500 pastors, Christian daycare for thousands of children, skills training for 2,000 indigent women, and a Christian school and college in Bangalore, India for 1,600 students.

Nathan is also a mentor to many Colorado business owners and a regular contributor of written devotionals for this group of CEOs. He is the former president of Retirement Planning Services, Inc. and its sister company 24HourFlex, firms that specialize in the consulting and administration of corporate, nonprofit, and governmental retirement and employee benefit plans in the Rocky Mountain region.

Nathan is a diligent student of the Word of God. This book is a culmination of forty years of notes, articles, and personal studies. He has often been asked to speak and teach on this topic.

Nathan is happily married to Jenny, his wife of thirty-eight years. They are parents to four wonderful adult children, and grandparents to thirteen delightful grandchildren, all of whom reside in beautiful Colorado.

He and his wife Jenny enjoy skiing, tennis, projects in their woodshop, playing their musical instruments and singing, and spending time with family, grandkids, and friends.

Nathan earned a masters in business administration from the University of Denver and a bachelors in music education from Oral Roberts University.

He can be contacted at nathan@fearofthelord.net. Visit the book's website at www.fearofthelord.net for Nathan's blog and other helpful resources.

ABOUT THE COVER

It's Not Just a Pretty Sunrise

O God, to the farthest corners of the planet people will stand in awe, startled and stunned by your signs and wonders. Sunrise brilliance and sunset beauty both take turns singing their songs of joy to you.[360]

As the eastern sky awakens from a steely blue to vibrant reds, and oranges and yellows creep across the sky enflaming clouds that were hidden in darkness, so our heart awakens from its slumber and springs forth worship of an awesome God whose mercies are new every morning.

It's not just a pretty sunrise. It's each morning's visual crescendo of worship, and every color expresses its own praise of its Creator in a harmonious, pulsating concerto that for now is muted to human ears because of sin yet is intended to inspire us to look up and join the morning song.

It's not just a pretty sunrise. It's a unique display of the beauty of a sky awash in color that is meant to startle our senses and cause us to fear the awesome greatness of our loving God who gifted this earth with a life-giving sun whose rays reveal beauty, provide strength, nourish our bodies, raise our hopes, and lift our spirits just like its Creator.

It's not just a pretty sunrise. It's creation's resplendent morning call to worship, and each call is a glorious one-and-only masterpiece painted across the sky and designed to elicit from us shouts of joyful thanksgiving to our gracious God who has once again chosen to bless us with the quickening rays of his sun.

It's not just a pretty sunrise.

ENDNOTES

1   Psalm 25:14 ESV.

2   Mayo Clinic Staff, "Friendships: Enrich Your Life and Improve Your Health," Mayo Clinic, April 24, 2019, https://www.mayoclinic.org/healthy-lifestyle/adult-health/in-depth/friendships/art-20044860.

3   Mark 14:36.

4   Curtis C. Mitchell, *Praying Jesus' Way* (Old Tappan, NJ: Revell, 1977), 65.

5   Galatians 4:6 NKJV.

6   Isaiah 30:18 BSB; brackets indicate my additions.

7   Deuteronomy 10:12.

8   Psalm 103:11.

9   Luke 22:33–34, 54–62.

10 John 21:1–17.

11 Lamentations 3:22–23.

12 Psalm 130:3–4 NLT.

13 Daniel Boorstin first coined this definition in his 1961 classic book, *The Image: A Guide to Pseudo-Events in America* (New York: Vintage Books, 1992; first published 1961).

14 *Matthew Henry's Complete Commentary on the Bible*, Isaiah 66:1–4, Studylight.org, accessed October 8, 2020, https://www.studylight.org/commentaries/mhm/isaiah-66.html#1.

15 Luke 12:5.

16 This passage is part of a prophecy concerning the Messiah who was yet to come, and it was fulfilled in Jesus the Christ.

17 Deuteronomy 5:29, emphasis added.

18 1 John 4:18. This passage is encouraging believers to have "confidence in the day of judgment" (v. 17). As believers, we have no reason to fear hell since the perfect love of Christ has driven out that fear from us. The passage is not instructing believers to cease fearing God.

19 Proverbs 2:1–5, emphasis added.

20 Psalm 25:14.

21 Deuteronomy 5:29, emphasis added.

22 Psalm 19:9.

23 Revelation 5:8, 14; 7:11; 19:4.

24 Revelation 15:4.

25 Revelation 14:7.

26 Luke 12:4–5.

27 Revelation 14:11; Mark 9:42–48; Revelation 20:10–15.

28 Philippians 2:12.

29 Some biblical scholars believe that the book of Job predates the Torah by as many as four hundred years. See, for example, Gleason L. Archer Jr., *A Survey of Old Testament Introduction*, revised ed. (Chicago, IL: Moody, 2007), 429–34; Roy B. Zuck, "Job," *The Bible Knowledge Commentary: Old Testament* (Wheaton, IL: Victor Books, 1985), 716–17.

30 Exodus 19:4–6.

31 Exodus 19:18–19.

32 Exodus 20:1–17.

33 Exodus 19:3–6; 20:6; Proverbs 3:12; Hebrews 12:6.

34 Exodus 20:19.

35 Exodus 20:20, emphasis added.

36 Joshua 2:11.

37 Isaiah 11:1–3, emphasis added.

38 Ephesians 1:4–5.

39 Ephesians 3:14–19.

40 Revelation 19:7; 21:2, 9.

41 Psalm 116:2.

42 Acts 5:1–11.

43 Psalm 23:3 ESV.

44 Hebrews 11:1.

45 Jenny Lee Riddle, "Revelation Song," Lyrics.com, STANDS4 LLC, 2020, accessed April 27, 2020, https://www.lyrics.com/lyric/30709367/Gateway+Worship.

46 Psalm 130:3–4 NASB, emphasis added.

47 Romans 8:15 NASB.

48 Proverbs 3:5–6.

49 Psalm 62:11–12.

50 Exodus 20:20, emphasis added.

51 Martin Luther, *Luther's Small Catechism* (St. Louis, MO: Concordia, 1986), section 1, "The First Commandment."

52 Philippians 2:12.

53 Janet Browne, *Charles Darwin: A Biography, Vol. 1–Voyaging*, reprint (Princeton, NJ: Princeton University Press, 1996), 47–48, 89–90.

54 Charles Darwin, *The Autobiography of Charles Darwin*, ed. Francis Darwin, public domain, emphasis added, https://a.co/4Z5HdJB.

55 Charles Darwin passed his Bachelor of Arts examinations at Christ's College in 1831. See "Charles Darwin's Education," Wikipedia,

accessed on June 13, 2020, https://en.wikipedia.org/wiki/Charles_
Darwin%27s_education.

56   "Religious Views of Charles Darwin," emphasis added, Wikipedia,
     accessed May 13, 2020, http://en.wikipedia.org/wiki/Religious_
     views_of_Charles_Darwin.

57   Adam Gopnik, *Angels and Ages: A Short Book about Darwin,
     Lincoln, and Modern Life* (New York: Vintage Books, 2009), 106.

58   Gopnik, *Angels and Ages*, 106.

59   Jerry Bergman, *The Darwin Effect* (Green Forest, AZ: Master Books,
     2014), 10.

60   Julian Young, *Friedrich Nietzsche: A Philosophical Biography* (New
     York: Cambridge University Press, 2010), 18.

61   Friedrich Nietzsche, *The Gay Science*, as quoted in Young, *Friedrich
     Nietzsche*, 239.

62   Young, *Friedrich Nietzsche*, 4.

63   Young, *Friedrich Nietzsche*, 5.

64   Bergman, *The Darwin Effect*, 292.

65   Bergman, *The Darwin Effect*, 290.

66   Bergman, *The Darwin Effect*, 291.

67   See Palash Ghosh, "How Many People Did Joseph Stalin Kill?,"
     International Business Times, March 3, 2013, https://www.ibtimes.
     com/how-many-people-did-joseph-stalin-kill-1111789.

68   2 Thessalonians 2:15.

69   Acts 9:1–4.

70   Philippians 3:4–6; Galatians 1:13–14; Acts 9:1–2; 22:3–5; 26:4–
     11.

71   Acts 7:54–8:3.

72   Acts 9:5.

73   Acts 9:5.

74 When Paul says in Acts 22:4, "I persecuted the followers of this Way to their death," we can take him at his word that he personally caused the deaths of these believers. He doesn't claim that he was only following orders from the high priest or that they died at the hands of others; rather, he takes personal responsibility for the deaths of those he persecuted. Further, in hindsight, he would be the first to admit that these believers were innocent of the charges leveled against them. Yet, he acted as judge, jury, and executioner, and this fits the definition of murder. Saul's transformation from terrorist and murderer to the most important author and missionary in church history is one of the greatest stories of God's grace.

75 Saul had a group traveling with him to Damascus for he knew that the attacks he was planning required a trained group to carry them out. The citizenry was commonly armed, and Jesus even encouraged his disciples to carry swords (Luke 22:36–38). So these attacks and arrests had to be carefully planned and executed for they had to assume that the individuals and groups they targeted would defend themselves.

76 Paul says in Acts 22:4 that he "persecuted followers of this Way to their death" and stoning was the means of execution, so we can safely assume that he participated in the stoning of these believers, for the accuser was required by law to cast the first stone (see John 8:1–11). Saul did not cast any stones in the stoning of Stephen because he was not one of the direct accusers (Acts 6:8–8:1).

77 I believe that Paul later used this event to develop the concept of the body of Christ (see 1 Corinthians 12:12–31). We are members of Christ's body, with him as the head. When Paul says in verse 26, "If one part suffers, every part suffers with it," I believe that he looked back to Jesus's words to him, "Why do you persecute me," as

the proof text of this truth. As the head of the body of Christ, Jesus experiences our pain and suffers with us.

78   Acts 6:8–8:1. Saul was certainly the ringleader of this group, for they laid their cloaks at his feet signifying his authority (Acts 7:58; 8:1; 22:20).

79   The lengthy and detailed transcription of Stephen's speech probably came from Paul (formerly Saul) who was present and was later a traveling companion of Luke who wrote the book of Acts.

80   Acts 7:60.

81   The fear of the Lord will correct false doctrine, for the lack of the fear of God is the genesis of false doctrine. Proverbs 9:10 says, "The fear of the Lord is the beginning of wisdom, and knowledge of the Holy One is understanding."

82   It would take years for Paul to fully develop his gospel, as he calls it in Romans 2:16: a righteousness that is by faith alone. Although we do not know the substance of Paul's sermons in these synagogues, Paul must have presented irrefutable proof from the Old Testament of the core truths: that Jesus was the Messiah, that his death was an atonement for our sins, that he rose from the dead as prophesied, and that he was now seated at the right hand of God.

83   Malachi 4:2 NASB.

84   Acts 9:10 NASB.

85   Acts 9:17–19 NASB.

86   Acts 9:20–25.

87   2 Corinthians 7:1, emphasis added.

88   Hebrews 5:7.

89   Luke 22:42 KJV.

90   Hebrews 5:8.

91   Proverbs 16:6.

92   Peter Carlson, "The Bible According to Thomas Jefferson," *The Humanist*, February 18, 2012, https://thehumanist.com/magazine/march-april-2012/features/the-bible-according-to-thomas-jefferson.

93   Exodus 20:20: "Moses said to the people, 'Do not be afraid. God has come to test you, so that the fear of God will be with you to keep you from sinning.'"

94   Genesis 1:1.

95   Isaiah 64:6 NET.

96   John 7:17.

97   Philippians 2:12–13.

98   John Bunyan, as quoted by Nicolas Batzig, "The Fear of Men," *Tabletalk Magazine*, Ligonier Ministries, October 1, 2013, https://www.ligonier.org/learn/articles/fear-men/.

99   James 5:16.

100   John 12:42.

101   1 Samuel 15:24.

102   Esther 3:1.

103   1 Kings 17:1.

104   1 Kings 18:21.

105   See 1 Kings 18:19, 40. Although Elijah gave instructions to "seize the prophets of Baal," it is assumed that all of the false prophets, including those of Asherah who had been assembled against Elijah on Mount Carmel, were killed that day.

106   Also known as Mount Sinai.

107   1 Kings 19:11–13, 15.

108   1 Kings 19:14.

109   1 Kings 19:18.

110   Luke 19:40.

111   Psalm 91:7.

112 Psalm 25:14.

113 Psalm 25:14.

114 God chose to take Elijah to heaven before these anointings could be completed. It was Elisha, not Elijah, who eventually anointed these two kings (2 Kings 8:7–15; 9:1–13).

115 Psalm 23:6.

116 Psalm 34:7 NASB.

117 Psalm 103:11, emphasis added.

118 Psalm 34:7.

119 2 Kings 1:12.

120 2 Kings 1:11–17.

121 Daniel 7:9–10.

122 Nehemiah 7:2.

123 Daniel 1:8–13.

124 Daniel 4.

125 Daniel 6.

126 Daniel 5.

127 Os Guinness, *The Call: Finding and Fulfilling God's Purpose for Your Life*, revised ed. (Nashville, TN: W Publishing, 2018), 107.

128 Genesis 39:6 NASB.

129 Genesis 39:9 NASB, emphasis added.

130 Psalm 139:7–10.

131 Genesis 45:8.

132 Genesis 50:19–21.

133 Psalm 103:11.

134 Ruth 1:16–17.

135 Ruth 2:1.

136 Ruth 2:20.

137 2 Corinthians 11:24–27.

138 2 Corinthians 5:11.

139 Philippians 3:13–15.

140 Eric Metaxas, *Martin Luther: The Man Who Rediscovered God and Changed the World* (New York: Penguin Books, 2017), 215–16.

141 Metaxas, *Martin Luther*, 40.

142 Metaxas, *Martin Luther*, 218.

143 Daniel 2:47.

144 It is unclear why Daniel was also not at this event. Perhaps he was ill or out of town at the time.

145 "How the Seven Wonders of the Ancient World Work," howstuffworks.com, accessed June 15, 2020, https://adventure. howstuffworks.com/seven-wonder-ancient-world2.htm.

146 Berosus (c. 280 bce), as quoted by the Jewish historian Josephus, *In Answer to Appion*, bk. 2.

147 Daniel 4:30–33.

148 Daniel 4:34.

149 Daniel 4:37.

150 Daniel 4:34.

151 Psalm 85:9.

152 Luke 23:39–43.

153 Luke 23:34.

154 Jim Bakker, as quoted by John Burton, "Todd Bentley Scandal Reveals Bigger Problem: 2 Demonic Spirits Roam the Church Freely," *Charisma News*, August 27, 2019, https://www. charismanews.com/opinion/77758-todd-bentley-scandal-reveals-bigger-problem-2-demonic-spirits-roam-the-church-freely.

155 Proverbs 3:34; James 4:6; 1 Peter 5:5.

156 1 Peter 3:15, emphasis added.

157 Psalm 24:1.

158 Psalm 67: 2, 7.

159 Psalm 67:7.

160 2 Corinthians 5:11.

161 Revelation 14:6–7, emphasis added.

162 Matthew 7:24–27.

163 James 1:22.

164 Hebrews 4:12.

165 *Our Daily Bread*, October 1, 1994, RBC Ministries (Grand Rapids, MI), used with permission.

166 Isaiah 55:9.

167 Genesis 22:1–2.

168 Genesis 22:12.

169 Proverbs 3:12; Hebrews 12:6.

170 Isaiah 50:10; Ecclesiastes 12:13. Emphasis added.

171 Exodus 20:19–20.

172 Psalm 118:4.

173 Genesis 4:1 ESV.

174 Psalm 139:23.

175 Psalm 25:12.

176 Ella Wheeler Wilcox, "Tis the Set of the Sail," Poetry Nook, accessed May 1, 2020, https://www.poetrynook.com/poem/tis-set-sail-or-one-ship-sails-east.

177 Philippians 2:12.

178 Proverbs 29:25.

179 Psalm 130:1–4 ESV, emphasis added.

180 Ephesians 1:7–8.

181 1 John 3:1.

182 Psalm 130:4 ESV.

183 Psalm 34:11.

184   Psalm 86:11.

185   Hebrews 12:2 ESV.

186   Psalm 139:16.

187   Matthew 6:24.

188   1 Timothy 6:10.

189   Colossians 3:17.

190   Mark 12:30.

191   Jeremiah 32:38–40, emphasis added.

192   Louis Pasteur, as quoted in *The Literary Digest* (October 18, 1902); see "Louis Pasteur," Wikiquote, accessed September 21, 2020, https://en.wikiquote.org/wiki/Louis_Pasteur.

193   According to Dr. Michael Eckelkamp, a Hebrew scholar, the Hebrew word translated "consider" could also be rendered "carefully examine," "deeply consider," "ponder over and over," or "diligently study." Literally, the original Hebrew reads "consider, consider." The Hebrew language did not contain emphatics that we use, such as underlining or boldface or italics. Instead, when the writer wished to bring special emphasis to a verb, he or she repeated it or augmented it or said it in a similar way.

194   Psalm 8:3–5.

195   Psalm 33:6–9.

196   Isaiah 40:25–26.

197   Job 38–41.

198   Job 38:4–11, 31–33; 39:1–3.

199   Mark 4:41.

200   Matthew 14:22–34.

201   Matthew 17:1–12.

202   Proverbs 2:5.

203   John 1:14.

204 Psalm 103:11.

205 The Decapolis was a large region of ten pagan gentile cities northeast of the Sea of Galilee. Hence, many people there owned and raised pigs that were forbidden in Israel proper. The city of Gerasa was one of these cities, and that's where the Gerasenes lived. See *The New Unger's Bible Dictionary*, by Merrill F. Unger, ed. R. K. Harrison (Chicago: Moody Press, 1988), s.vv. "Decapolis," "Gerasene."

206 Mark 5:1–20.

207 Mark 7:31–37.

208 Psalm 40:1–3, emphasis added.

209 Psalm 130:4 ESV.

210 Psalm 86:11.

211 Ephesians 5:18–19.

212 Psalm 40:3.

213 Hebrews 12:28.

214 Jonah 1:16. Apparently, Jonah reconnected with these sailors at a later time to capture the "rest of the story" from their perspective because, at this point in the story, he was underwater and sinking fast.

215 Jonah 2:4–6.

216 Jonah 2:9.

217 Exodus 14:31.

218 Exodus 15:11 NASB.

219 Daniel 4:3.

220 Daniel 4:34.

221 Isaiah 6:1, 4.

222 Isaiah 6:5 NASB.

223 Isaiah 9:6.

224 Matthew 14:33.

225 Revelation 14:6–7.

226 Revelation 15:3–4.

227 Exodus 4:30–31.

228 God gave Moses a third sign—the pouring out of Nile water that turned into blood, but it is unclear if he used this sign at this time with the Hebrew people.

229 John 7:37–38.

230 Revelation 22:13.

231 Hebrews 12:2.

232 John 6:35; Matthew 14:33; Daniel 7:9.

233 Revelation 14:14.

234 Isaiah 7:14; Luke 2:11; Isaiah 9:6.

235 Job 19:25 NASB; Revelation 22:16; John 11:25; Revelation 19:16 ESV.

236 John 7:39.

237 Ephesians 5:18–20, emphasis added.

238 Leviticus 23:37.

239 2 Samuel 23:13–17.

240 John 4:7–24.

241 Glenn Packiam, *Discover the Mystery of Faith* (Colorado Springs, CO: David C. Cook, 2013), loc. 1070 of 1431, Kindle.

242 Hebrews 12:28–29, emphasis added.

243 Psalm 100:4.

244 Psalm 5:7.

245 Psalm 2:11 ESV.

246 Psalm 139:14; 63:3, 7; 7:17; Luke 1:68. Emphasis added.

247 Psalm 89:15.

248 Psalm 69:34.

249 Psalm 68:32–33.

250 Jeremiah 10:6–7.

251 Mary Maclean, vocalist and songwriter, "Creator King," track 2 on *Beyond*, Upswing Music, 2010, used with permission.

252 Psalm 24:3–4.

253 Hebrews 4:16.

254 Psalm 5:7.

255 Psalm 108:4.

256 Psalm 89:5–8.

257 Ephesians 5:18–19.

258 Hebrews 12:28, emphasis added.

259 Mark 10:46–52.

260 Mark 3:1–6.

261 Luke 7:11–17.

262 1 Corinthians 13:13.

263 Nathan Carlson, "Cory," composed in 2017.

264 John 11:33–35; 19:25–27.

265 2 Corinthians 5:17.

266 Job 6:14 NASB.

267 1 John 4:8.

268 My heartfelt thanks to my good friend and Bible scholar Malcolm Smith for this wonderful teaching.

269 Job 2:9–10.

270 Psalm 145:3 NASB; Isaiah 55:9.

271 Proverbs 1:25–29.

272 Proverbs 19:3 ESV.

273 Jeremiah 5:20–24.

274 Michael G. Strauss, PhD, *The Creator Revealed: A Physicist Examines the Big Bang and the Bible* (Bloomington, IN: Westbow Press, 2018), 52.

275 Strauss, *The Creator Revealed*, 50.

276 Strauss, *The Creator Revealed*, 47.

277 Strauss, *The Creator Revealed*, 51.

278 Hugh Ross, "Part 2. Fine-Tuning for Intelligent Physical Life," Appendix C in *Why the Universe Is the Way It Is* (Grand Rapids, MI: Baker Books, 2008), http://d4bge0zxg5qba.cloudfront.net/files/compendium/compendium_part2.pdf.

279 Psalm 33:6–10.

280 Job 6:14.

281 Researchers are now discovering that the best-run companies are those that are led by a humble leader, and those companies who fail often have at the helm a leader filled with pride and hubris. Read Jim Collins's excellent books *Good to Great* (New York: HarperCollins, 2001) and his follow-up book, *How the Mighty Fall: And Why Some Companies Never Give In* (New York: HarperCollins, 2009).

282 Numbers 12:3; Luke 1:48 NASB; Zechariah 9:9 NASB; Matthew 11:29 NASB.

283 2 Chronicles 7:14; James 4:10; Philippians 2:8 NKJV. Emphasis added.

284 When human beings defy God's path of humility, he will sometimes step in and humble the individual. Such was the case with King Nebuchadnezzar whom God humbled after the ruler refused to do that himself (Daniel 4).

285 Philippians 2:7–8.

286 1 Corinthians 2:2–3.

287 2 Corinthians 12:7, 10.

288 James 4:6 NASB.

289 Philippians 2:13.

290 C. S. Lewis, *The Screwtape Letters* (San Francisco: Harper San Francisco, 1942), 70.

291 Psalm 139:17–18; 130:4; Luke 1:50; Psalm 89:2; 33:6; 147:4.

292 Isaiah 6:1–8 NASB; Matthew 17:1–8.

293 Revelation 1:12–18; Luke 5:1–11 NASB.

294 Deuteronomy 5:29.

295 Job 1:1; cf. v. 8.

296 Acts 10:1–8 NASB.

297 Acts 10:9–23 NASB.

298 Acts 10:23–48 NASB.

299 Acts 1–2.

300 Psalm 141:2.

301 Philippians 2:3–4.

302 Job 29:11–13.

303 Go to www.indiatransformed.org. Proceeds from this book are being donated to this ministry. I serve on the board of directors of India Transformed.

304 James 1:27.

305 Matthew 7:17.

306 Napoleon Bonaparte, "Napoleon's Last Will and Testament," April 15, 1821, Napoleon.org, https://www.napoleon.org/en/history-of-the-two-empires/articles/napoleons-last-will-and-testament/.

307 Deuteronomy 5:29.

308 Exodus 20:20; Proverbs 16:6.

309 Psalm 34:9.

310 Psalm 34:7; 103:13; 128; 111:10; Luke 1:50; Proverbs 22:4.

311 Proverbs 19:23; Psalm 103:13.

312 Proverbs 14:27; 16:6.

313 Proverbs 9:10; Ephesians 5:21.

314 Deuteronomy 5:29; Philippians 2:12; Psalm 34:7.

315 Hebrews 12:28–29.

316 John 7:17.

317 Jonah 4:11.

318 Proverbs 9:10.

319 2 Timothy 3:16; 2 Peter 1:20–21; Psalm 119:142, 151, 160.

320 Proverbs 2:1–6; Matthew 4:4; Romans 12:1–2; 1 Corinthians 2:10–16; 2 Corinthians 3:17–18.

321 Psalm 1:1–3; 37:30–31; 119:11.

322 Psalm 19. Also refer to resources by Christian authors such as Strauss, *The Creator Revealed*; Lee Strobel, *The Case for a Creator: A Journalist Investigates Scientific Evidence That Points toward God* (Grand Rapids, MI: Zondervan, 2004); J. I. Packer, *Knowing God* (Downers Grove, IL: InterVarsity Press, 1973); A. W. Tozer, *The Knowledge of the Holy* (San Francisco: Harper & Row, 1961); and C. Samuel Storms, *The Grandeur of God: A Theological and Devotional Study of the Divine Attributes* (Grand Rapids, MI: Baker Book House, 1984).

323 Proverbs 22:4.

324 Hebrews 12:28; Psalm 2:11.

325 For example, see the story of Cornelius in Acts 10; also note Psalm 1:1–3; 119:97–100, 103–104; Matthew 25:34–40; Luke 14:12–14; 2 Corinthians 8:1–15; and James 1:27.

326 Psalm 25:14; 139:17–18; 103:11.

327 Luke 2:52.

328 Mark 6:1–6.

329   For the background to this ancient practice, see Exodus 13:2 and Leviticus 12:1–4.

330   Luke 2:25–35.

331   Micah 5:2; Isaiah 7:14; 9:1–2, 7.

332   Luke 2:35.

333   Luke 1:46–55, emphasis added.

334   Isaiah 11:2–3.

335   Luke 2:52.

336   Psalm 147:10–11.

337   Romans 8:29; Galatians 5:22–23.

338   Psalm 34:11.

339   For an outstanding marriage seminar, consider attending a Weekend to Remember seminar by FamilyLife.org.

340   On this I especially recommend Dr. Tedd Tripp's book, *Shepherding a Child's Heart* (Wapwallopen, PA: Shepherd Press, 1995).

341   1 Samuel 7:12.

342   For example, see Deuteronomy 4:10; 5:15; 7:18; 8:2, 18; 9:7.

343   Luke 22:19.

344   Psalm 77:11.

345   Lamentations 3:22–23 ESV.

346   Psalm 103:11.

347   See the article on a hand-written Torah known as a Sefer Torah, accessed July 24, 2020, https://en.wikipedia.org/wiki/Sefer_Torah. The Torah consists of the first five books of the Bible: Genesis, Exodus, Leviticus, Numbers, and Deuteronomy.

348   Deuteronomy 17:18–20, emphasis added.

349   Malachi 3:16–17.

350   Psalm 34:7.

351   Revelation 14:7; see also 15:3–4.

352   Isaiah 33:5–6.

353   James 1:17 ESV.

354   Psalm 34:11 ESV.

355   Psalm 19:9.

356   Philippians 4:8.

357   Revelation 14:6–7, emphasis added.

358   Psalm 103:8.

359   Proverbs 31:30.

360   Psalm 65:8 TPT.

A free ebook edition is available with the purchase of this book.

To claim your free ebook edition:

Visit MorganJamesBOGO.com
Sign your name CLEARLY in the space
Complete the form and submit a photo of
the entire copyright page
You or your friend can download the ebook
to your preferred device

Morgan James
BOGO™

A **FREE** ebook edition is available for you
or a friend with the purchase of this print book.

CLEARLY SIGN YOUR NAME ABOVE

Instructions to claim your free ebook edition:
1. Visit MorganJamesBOGO.com
2. Sign your name CLEARLY in the space above
3. Complete the form and submit a photo
   of this entire page
4. You or your friend can download the ebook
   to your preferred device

Print & Digital Together Forever.

Snap a photo

Free ebook

Read anywhere